This page is intentionally left blank.

SCRUM MANAGEMENT:

A Day In The Life Of...

Product Owner

Scrum
Management:

A Day In The Life Of...

Product Owner

Aligned with the PMBOK® Sixth Edition

PMBOK Guide is a registered mark of Project Management Institute, Inc.

This page is intentionally left blank.

ISBN-13: 978-1724006332

ISBN-10: 1724006339

Table of Contents

List of Figures

List of Tables

1 Why Should You Care About Scrum?

You've heard about Scrum. But, frankly, why should you care? Why should you add this product development methodology to your already jam-packed toolbox? Why?

Well, you should care about Scrum because:

- Scrum is not an excuse for not having well-defined development and quality management processes
- Scrum is not that easy to deploy and adopt
- Scrum is not for everyone and for every team
- Scrum doesn't manage your main assets: your people
- Scrum is not the magic bullet to all problems

Alright, agreed, it might not the best way to explain why you should care about Scrum. Let me try again:

- Scrum is an Agile Framework designed to manage and control product development (and not only software) through lightweight iterative and incremental practices
- Scrum is about common sense
- Scrum is about using what works and discarding what doesn't
- Scrum is about increasing productivity, and reducing time to benefits, and most importantly,
- Scrum is about empowering the team to focus on the task at hand

Still on the fence? Really? Common! You probably do care, and because you do, you should care about this book too.

In the **Scrum Management:** *The Agile Practitioners Survival Guide*, I provided you with the baseline foundation to understand the Agile values and principles. I also described how to survive in a Scrum environment, discussing the people, processes, artifacts and ceremonies; in other words, the Survival Guide gave you the building blocks that are required to apply Scrum to your projects and product development. So, why should you care about this second volume?

You see Scrum is like cooking. You may have the ingredients to the desired recipe, and you can probably follow the instructions to cook a decent dish. But, can you honestly call yourself a cordon bleu, a master chief? You can't, right? In fact, if you do, you'll be quickly chopped! Not a pleasant outcome.

Remember that the objective of my first book was simple: *survive!* And in order to survive, I listed and described all the necessary ingredients. I then laid out the steps to execute Scrum from submitting a Backlog Item, grooming the Product Backlog, planning a Release and Sprint, to executing the Sprint, and learning from the completed iteration via the Sprint Review and Retrospective. But I didn't, *purposely*, dive deep into the recipe and illustrated what distinguishes a cook from a master chief.

Why did I do it on purpose? Because I didn't want you to run before walking. Expertise develops daily, not in a day. And rising to a higher level of expertise requires time and practical experience! And this is where this book comes into play!

This book is indeed written to help you start jogging, run, and cross the finish line. To achieve this objective, I'll **guide you through the Scrum Framework,** looking at it **from the Product Owner's eyes**. And to get off on the right foot, let us first do a brief recap of Scrum framework.

Sounds like a good plan?

So, without further due, let's dive in!

2 The Crash Course on Scrum

This chapter discusses the Scrum Framework and its typical timeline, and comes back on the Responsibility Assignment Matrices introduced in the **Scrum Management**: *The Agile Practitioners Survival Guide[1]*.

2.1 The Framework

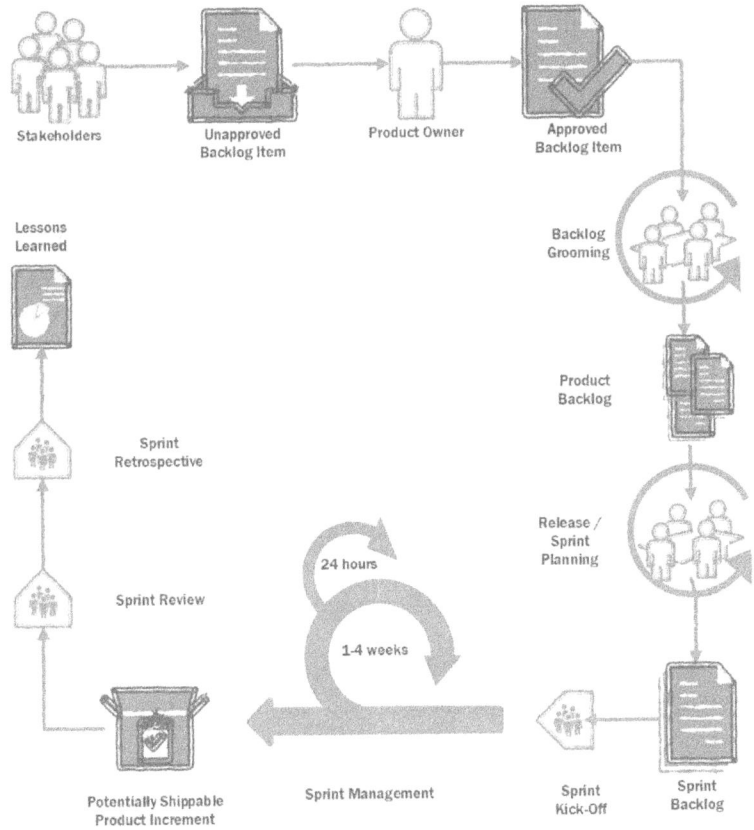

FIGURE 1: THE SCRUM FRAMEWORK

---

[1] Scrum Management: The Agile Practitioners Survivor Guide is available here: https://amzn.to/2ERcMP6

Scrum is first and foremost a framework that effectively links people and processes, via a well-defined set of ceremonies and the appropriate use of technology. This is how it works...

1) Anyone can submit new requirements, requests for change, or variances to resolve in the form of a User Story.

2) The product owner triages the submitted user stories. This means the product owner needs to determine the cohesiveness of each one; as such s/he can either drop a User Story with a comment or label (e.g.: not applicable, already resolved, duplicate request, question requiring simply an answer, etc.), or approve it and assign a business priority.

3) The product owner and the solution lead(s) then meet during the Backlog Grooming session to review the submitted and approved user stories. During the Backlog Grooming session (or subsequent estimation meetings), each approved User Story is estimated and provided with a certain weight (or Story Point), and places it into the Product Backlog for the Scrum team to consider during the next Sprint Planning meeting.

4) The Scrum team meets during the Sprint Planning to review the Product Backlog. In this ceremony, the Scrum team decomposes the User Story into smaller pieces of work (backlog items and Sprint tasks), and creates the Sprint Backlog.

5) The Scrum master then schedules a Sprint Kick-Off meeting. During the Kick-Off, the Scrum master and the Scrum team review and validate the User Story decomposition, ensuring each Backlog Item Acceptance Criteria is clear and understood by all. It's time to get to work! It's time to execute the Sprint.

6) During the Sprint execution, the Scrum team and Scrum master meet daily. In the Daily Scrum, each team member answers 3 simple questions: what did they do yesterday? What do they plan on working on? And what impediments do they face?

7) At the end of the Sprint, the Scrum team invites all product stakeholders to demonstrate and discuss the completed Potentially

Shippable Product Increments. The Scrum team also conducts a Sprint Retrospective to capture any lessons learned: what went well, what did not go as planned, what could be improved, or re-applied.

2.2 The Timeline

Because every problem must be appropriately framed before finding a viable solution, in this section, we'd assume the following (a) the Sprint duration is two weeks, and (b) all product stakeholders begin their workday at 9a.m. and end it at 5pm. I know, it sounds too perfect to be true, but, we'll deviate from this ideal world in later sections. So, for now, bear with me, and take a look at the below calendar.

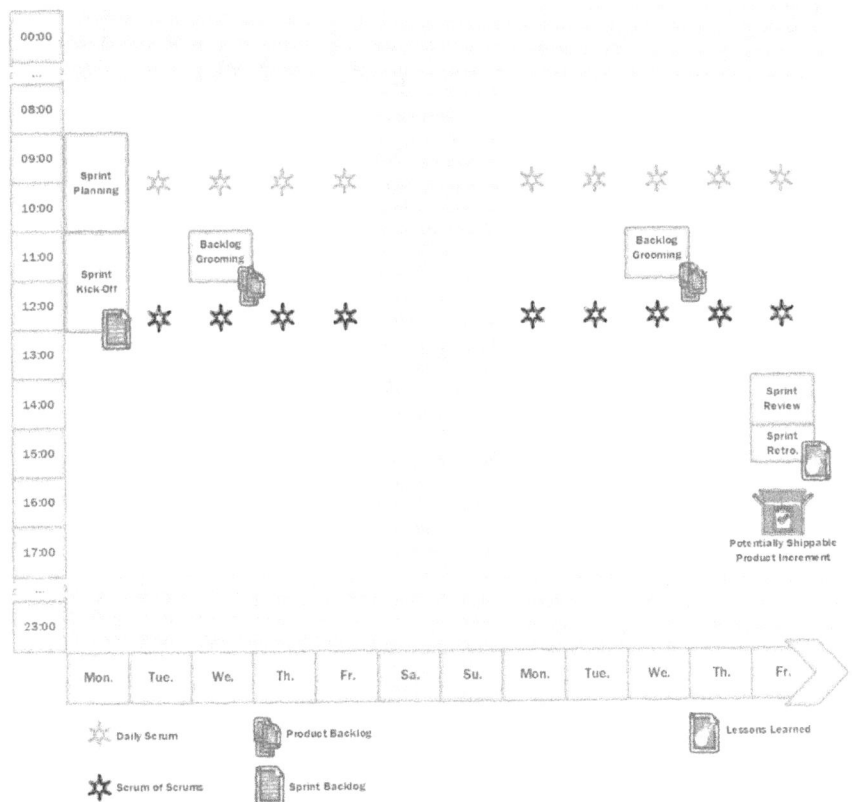

FIGURE 2: THE SCRUM TIMELINE

Week	Day	Time	Description
//1	Mon.	09:00	Welcome everyone to this bright and sunny day! We start the week with the Sprint Planning where all product stakeholders are invited. Together, we review the business priorities, set a goal for the new Sprint, and identify a list of Product Backlog Items that could possibly be delivered in two weeks.
		11:00	The Scrum team has already a defined sprint goal. So, it's time to kick-off the Sprint!
			In the next 2 hours, the team, guided by the Scrum master, is going to determine a way to achieve this goal. Here are the steps: First, the team assesses its capacity to deliver a certain number of Story Points. Second, the team reviews the Product Backlog Items identified earlier, and breaks them down into smaller pieces, into Sprint tasks that can be completed in 4 to 16 hours. The Scrum team then agrees on a defined list of prioritized Product Backlog Items to deliver: the Sprint Backlog is defined.
			The Scrum master invites the product owner to re-join the Sprint Kick-off for the Scrum team to present the backlog items they commit to deliver at the end of the Sprint.
			The Sprint is now officially kicked-off: Let's get to work!

Week	Day	Time	Description
	Tue.	10:00	Yesterday, the Scrum team spent an entire afternoon defining the Sprint Backlog. Today, the team and the Scrum master meet for their first daily stand-up to self-organize the committed scope of work for the Sprint. This is the Daily Scrum. Every team member is required to attend and answer three simple questions: 1) What did you do yesterday? 2) What are you going to do today? 3) What impediments are in your way? The product owner, project manager(s), manager(s) and any other product stakeholder(s) may attend the Daily Scrum, but only as observers. They can only listen.
		12:00	Scrum of Scrums! This optional daily meeting is typically held (a) when a product development team gets bigger than 10 members, (b) when different groups or teams across the company are engaged in the product development effort, (c) when teams are located in different countries and multiple time zones and that activities must be coordinated to deliver a product or a particular feature. The Scrum of Scrums is theoretically held after all the participating Scrum teams have conducted their own Daily Scrum and designated a representative who is most knowledgeable or has the most insights into the current inter-team dependencies

Week	Day	Time	Description
			and impediments, or continuous integration needs.
			During the Scrum of Scrums, each team representative answers the following questions:
			1) What are the risks, inter-team dependencies or impediments your team resolved yesterday?
			2) What are the risks, inter-team dependencies or impediments your team plans to work on today?
			3) What are the new risks, inter-team dependencies or impediments in your team way?
	Wed.	10:00	Daily Scrum
		11:00	Backlog Grooming!
			First, there is no established protocol on how to conduct Backlog Grooming. In my opinion, this meeting can be facilitated by the product owner and attended by the Solution Lead(s); I don't think having the entire team participating is required. The team will surely have legion of opportunities later on to review and discuss the approved Product Backlog Items.
			And so, once a week, the attendees analyze, detail or slice the submitted user stories, as well as prioritize the Product Backlog. When feasible, the attendees can provide a Story Point estimate to the reviewed backlog items. The end goal of the Backlog Grooming is to simplify the

Week	Day	Time	Description
			next Sprint Planning.
		12:00	*(optional) Scrum of Scrums*
	Thu.	10:00	Daily Scrum
		12:00	*(optional) Scrum of Scrums*
	Fri.	10:00	Daily Scrum
		12:00	*(optional) Scrum of Scrums*
	Sat. Sun.		It's time for all to enjoy the weekend! Spend time with your loved ones, explore the city, and its attractions. Get out and relax in the rain, sunshine or snow. Enjoy your life. Go for a run. Live. And don't forget to laugh and smile!
//2	Mon.	10:00	Daily Scrum
		12:00	*(optional) Scrum of Scrums*
	Tue.	10:00	Daily Scrum
		12:00	*(optional) Scrum of Scrums*
	Wed.	10:00	Daily Scrum
		11:00	Backlog Grooming
		12:00	*(optional) Scrum of Scrums*
	Thu.	10:00	Daily Scrum
		12:00	*(optional) Scrum of Scrums*
	Fri.	10:00	Daily Scrum
		12:00	*(optional) Scrum of Scrums*
		14:00	Can you believe it? The Sprint is about to end. The team worked hard the past two weeks to achieve the agreed sprint goal.

Week	Day	Time	Description
			This early afternoon, all the product stakeholders meet to review what has been completed. During the Sprint Review, the attendees are probed and encouraged to ask questions about the developed features and provide feedback. They discuss the environmental factors that may influence the developed product increments. They can recommend enhancements or new features so that the product can best adapt to the constantly evolving business needs.
		15:00	Immediately following the Sprint Review, the Scrum master, the Scrum team and the product owner dive into the development processes so that the future Sprints can be more effective, efficient, and produce higher quality product increments. During the Sprint Retrospective, the attendees document the following: (a) What went well? (b) What did not go so well? And (c) What could be improved?
		17:00	Before leaving the office for a well-deserved weekend, the product owner reviews the Potentially Shippable Product Increments delivered by the team, and accepts or rejects them. To ship or not to ship.

TABLE 1: SCRUM TIMELINE

2.3   The Responsibility Assignment Matrix

As discussed in the **Scrum Management**: *The Agile Practitioners Survival Guide*, one key foundational principle of Scrum is having Self-Organizing Teams. This means that sentences such as *"it's not my job"* should never be said or heard. But, we are all humans... And so, when self-organization is central to the successful delivery of a project, product, or service, everyone involved in the product development is a vital piece of the same puzzle, and should understand its respective role and responsibilities. Knowing who is the owner (or accountable person) of a particular step in the development process reduces confusion, miscommunication, and facilitates the resolution of issues, conflicts, or disagreements. This is where a Responsibility Assignment Matrix (RAM) comes handy in clarifying one's duties.

"A Responsibility Assignment Matrix (RAM), also known as RACI matrix or Linear Responsibility Chart (LRC), describes the participation by various roles in completing tasks or deliverables for a project or business process. It is especially useful in clarifying roles and responsibilities in cross-functional/departmental projects and processes." (Wikipedia)

RACI stands for:
- **R**esponsible: They do the work and actively contribute to the process output or deliverable
- **A**ccountable: They are the ultimate decision-maker in accepting the process output or generated deliverable and product increment
- **C**onsulted: They contribute to the decision-making process by providing their inputs, which may or may not be considered in the produced end-result
- **I**nformed: They are kept up-to-date on the decisions, process outputs, sprint progress, deliverable and product increment

The first table presents the RACI for the Scrum Artifacts, while the second table shows the RACI for the Scrum Ceremonies.

The Artifacts	The Customer	The End-User	The Product Owner	The Scrum Master	The Solution Lead	The Scrum Team	The Stakeholder	The Manager	The Project Manager
User Story	R	R	R/A	R	R	R	R	I	R
Product Backlog	C	C	R/A	R	C	R	C	I	C
Product Vision	C	C	R/A	I	C	I	C	I	I
Backlog Item	R	R	R/A	R	R	R	R	I	R
Sprint Task	I	I	I	C	C	R/A	I	I	I
Definition of Done	I	I	C	R/A	C	R	I	C	C
Estimation									
Story Point Estimate	I	I	R/A	C	R	C	I	I	I
Level of Effort (Hours) Estimate	I	I	I	C	C	R/A	I	I	I
Sprint Goal	C	C	R/A	R	C	R	C	I	C
Sprint Backlog	I	I	C	R	C	R/A	I	I	I
Sprint Burndown	I	I	I	R	I	R/A	I	I	I
Scrum Task Board	I	I	I	R	I	R/A	I	I	I
Potentially Shippable Product Increment	C/I	I	R/A	R	C/I	R	I	I	I
Lessons Learned	I	I	R	R/A	I	R	I	I	I

R: Responsible; A: Accountable; C: Consulted; I: Informed

TABLE 2: SCRUM ARTIFACTS RACI MATRIX

The Ceremonies	The Customer	The End-User	The Product Owner	The Scrum Master	The Solution Lead	The Scrum Team	The Stakeholder	The Manager	The Project Manager
Backlog Grooming	C	C	R/A	C	R	C	C	I	C
Estimation Meetings	I	I	R/A	R	R	R	I	I	I
Release Planning	C	I	R/A	C	C	C	C	I	R
Sprint Planning (Part 1)	C	C	R/A	R	C	R	C	I	C
Sprint Kick-Off (Sprint Planning Part 2)	I	I	C	R	C	R/A	I	I	I
Daily Scrum	C/I	C/I	C/I	R	C/I	R/A	I	I	C/I
Scrum of Scrums	C/I	C/I	C/I	R	C/I	R/A	I	I	C/I
Sprint Review	R	R	R/A	R	R	R	R	R	R
Sprint Retrospective	I	I	R	R	I	R/A	I	I	I

R: *Responsible*; A: *Accountable*; C: *Consulted*; I: *Informed*

TABLE 3: SCRUM CEREMONIES RACI MATRIX

The previous RACI matrices were introduced in the **Scrum Management**: *The Agile Practitioners Survival Guide*.

This second book goes one step further, and dives into each critical role, providing practical tips in applying Scrum in your day-to-day job.

3   A Day in the Life of... The Product Owner

Yes! You are now officially the manager of a product being envisioned, developed and adapted through the Scrum Development processes. This means that you are the product owner. Congratulations! Alas, there is no time to waste. The celebrations will have to wait until... well, until you know what to do! But, don't you worry! Take a breath, take in the fresh air, and get ready to be cranked up! We have plenty to talk about and cover so that you transition successfully into your new role, so that you can understand and master your responsibilities.

3.1   Understand the Product Owner Role

Without a good product owner, the Scrum team has no chance of building and delivering a product that will satisfy the customer requirements. And when a product fails to meet the customer expectations, when a product misses the mark, the product is unlikely to cross the chasm, and the company fails to attain its business and financial goals. As such, the product owner has a pivotal role in the product and company successes. But what does the product owner actually do to contribute to success?

First and foremost, the product owner represents the customers. You know the old adage: *"the Customer is King."* Well, you see, on one hand, this is true. You need customers to purchase your product, and if the product doesn't consider or meet the customer needs and expectations, it'll never fly off the shelves, right? On the other hand, it doesn't mean that everything the customer wants, it gets.

Let me explain that through a very simple example.

Peter works for an American automaker. While exhibiting the latest prototype of a self-driving car at the Paris Motor Show (*Le Mondial de l'Automobile*), several French customers agree to purchase a model but only if the car operates on the meters and km/h system. If you were Peter, would you immediately follow-up and instruct the product team to only support the metrics system? Of course not!

You would not blindly implement what your French customers ask you to do. Instead, you'd wonder why they demand such change, and then request the product team to support displaying distance and speed using different measurement systems.

This sounds rather simple, doesn't it? Well, it's not always that easy!

As the product owner, it's your role and responsibility to understand who your customers are, what they want and why. Armed with these unique customer insights, you are tasked to establish the product vision and articulate the requirements so that your product meets or exceeds the customer wants. A good product owner is, therefore, someone who can communicate and collaborate with a wide-range of personalities; customers are rarely easy to work with, and they are rarely – not to say never – please! Hence, you must be good – excellent - at working with people, managing conflicts and engaging in difficult conversations.

In Scrum, the requirements are documented as User Stories and managed through the Product Backlog. This well-defined structure should help you balance competing business priorities, and deal with opposing or changing requirements. As the product owner, one of your main responsibilities is to manage the Product Backlog by collecting, triaging, detailing, clarifying and prioritizing each submitted product backlog item. And you must be able to do all of these (and more) while collaborating and negotiating with both internal and external stakeholders.

Your industry knowledge, domain expertise, and customer insights will enable you to develop the product roadmap and ensure the evolving market needs are addressed by the next and future releases. In this critical planning exercise, you must consider and weigh-in the business value of each product backlog item. The same attention should be given to the preparation and definition of the goal for the next iteration. Remember that, in the end, you are and will be held accountable for the return on investment (ROI) of the product. And, this is why you need to always maximize the value of your product and optimize the work done by the product development team(s). The bottom line, in layman's terms, is that you must strive for getting the biggest bang for the buck! Yes, I've never said it was easy to be the product owner, did I?

Naturally, your role as product owner doesn't stop with the planning of a release and sprint. Your role extends to the development of each product increment. You represent the voice of the customer, own the Product Backlog, and assist the Scrum team understanding the in-and-out of product backlog items to be built and delivered. Throughout the Sprint execution, you work closely with the Scrum master and product stakeholders to remove the impediments preventing the Scrum team to achieve the agreed sprint goal. You also shield the Scrum team from any external interruptions and disturbances; whatever happens inside or outside the organization should not affect the Scrum team. The team is to focus on the committed Sprint backlog; and that's already plenty for the team to handle!

Last but not least, don't forget that the product owner is accountable for accepting each potentially shippable product increment. This means that you should carefully review the acceptance criteria of each submitted product backlog item so that there is no confusion to validate the developed requirement. You should as well review regularly the Definition of *Done* so that the overall quality of shipped product meets or exceeds your customer expectations.

Long story short, the product owner is responsible for the following tasks:
- Establish the Product Vision
  o Define your Business Model
  o Articulate the Problem Statement
  o Ideate Product Vision Statements
  o Validate your Product Vision
- Determine the Product Themes
- Determine the Product Epics
- Develop the Product Personas
- Work with the Scrum Master
- Manage the Product Backlog
  o Collect the Product Requirements
  o Assist in the User Stories refinement
  o Triage the Submitted Backlog Item
  o Groom the Product Backlog
  o Prioritize the Product Backlog

- Define the Minimum Viable Product
- Plan the Next Product Release (using User Story Mapping)
  - Assist in Establishing the Product Roadmap
  - Establish the Short to Mid-term Product Roadmap
  - Establish the Long-term Product Roadmap
- Manage the Sprint
  - Define the Sprint Goal
  - Prepare the Sprint
  - Review the Sprint Backlog
  - Shield the Scrum team during the Sprint
  - Represent the Voice of the Customer
  - Assist the Scrum team during the Sprint
  - Evaluate the Sprint
    - Terminate the Sprint
    - Review the Sprint Burndown Chart
    - Review the Sprint Burnup Chart
    - Evaluate the Sprint Velocity
  - Inspect and Adapt the Potentially Shippable Product Increments
  - Learn from the Past Sprint
- Monitor the Release
- Drive the Product Quality Requirements
  - Manage the Technical Debt
  - Manage the Definition of Done
- Avoid the Common Mistakes
- Have a Balanced Life

The next sections will delve further into each task. But before deep-diving, let us get one last high-level look at the product owner's responsibilities as presented by the RACI matrix on the next page:

The Product Owner

The Artifacts

Artifact	
User Story	R/A
Product Backlog	R/A
Product Vision	R/A
Backlog Item	R/A
Sprint Task	I
Definition of Done	C
Estimation	
Story Point Estimate	R/A
Level of Effort (Hours) Estimate	I
Sprint Goal	R/A
Sprint Backlog	C
Sprint Burndown	I
Scrum Task Board	I
Potentially Shippable Product Increment	R/A
Lessons Learned	R

The Ceremonies

Ceremony	
Backlog Grooming	R/A
Estimation Meetings	R/A
Release Planning	R/A
Sprint Planning (Part 1)	R/A
Sprint Kick-Off (Sprint Planning Part 2)	C
Daily Scrum	C/I
Scrum of Scrums	C/I
Sprint Review	R/A
Sprint Retrospective	R

Legend:
- **R:** *Responsible*
- **A:** *Accountable*
- **C:** *Consulted*
- **I:** *Informed*

TABLE 4: PRODUCT OWNER'S RACI MATRIX

3.2   Establish the Product Vision

Before anything, you need a vision for the product you want to build. You need a vision, a clear direction that would inspire the entire team to innovate, design, build and deliver the next iPhone, the next Tesla, the thing big thing! If you don't believe a clear vision is critical to succeed, think of Neil Armstrong.

Why did he become the first person to walk on the moon? Why did the United States send him 238,900 miles away from Earth? What inspired an entire nation to even go to the Moon?

On May 25, 1961, President John F. Kennedy announced before the Congress the dramatic and ambitious goal of sending an American safely to the Moon before the end of the decade. He had a vision and communicated it so clearly that it captured America's attention and imagination. His message energized scientists, engineers, and everyone else involved in the nation's Apollo program to actualize this vision. And on July 21, 1969, less than eight years after Kennedy's announcement, Neil Armstrong made the first step on the lunar surface and told the world the now famous words:

> *"That's one small step for man, one giant leap for mankind."*

You see, it's the same thing for a company or a person who creates a vision for a new product. Having an idea is a great start but, this single step isn't enough. The journey to creating a product always begins with a vibrant and distinct picture, which tells a unique and compelling story. People are drawn to such vision.

In the **Scrum Management**: *The Agile Practitioners Survival Guide*, I explained the following:

A Product Vision is a statement describing an overarching goal that inspires and drives people to design and create the product. The Product Vision statement should also answer several key questions:
- Who is the customer?

- What and why does s/he want?
- What is the market offering now?
- What is wrong with the existing offers?
- And, how could your product fix this?

Hence, the product is the outcome, the concrete implementation of the Product Vision. And, while there are many ways to write a Product Vision statement, a generally adopted format comes from *"Crossing the Chasm"* by Geoffrey Moore:

- **For** [target customer]
- **Who** [statement of the need]
- **The** [Product Name] is a [Product Category]
- **That** [key benefit, compelling reason to buy].
- **Unlike** [primary competitive alternative],
- **Our Product** [statement of primary differentiation].

Despite of the efficacy of Geoffrey Moore's general template, Simon Sinek, best-selling author of *"Start with Why,"* has a different take on how to write a Product Vision, explaining why some companies inspire millions of customers to purchase their products while others don't. It all narrows down to the fact that successful companies communicate differently, they communicate from the inside out. They articulate their beliefs, explain their key differentiators, and then describe their product as listed below:

- Why: This is the core belief of the business. It's why the business exists.
- How: This is how the business fulfills that core belief.
- What: This is what the company does to fulfill that core belief: the product.

In the end, a Product Vision statement should be able to sustain itself through time and change (internal and external). A *good* Product Vision should avoid misinterpretation, be clear and concise, focus on the delivered experience, and guide and motivate everyone to build and purchase the product.

All of that is great information, but, let's translate this into small actionable steps you can take to articulate the product vision for an existing product or a product that has yet to be built.

First, ask yourself the following questions:
- Who are your customers?
- Who has used it, who is using it, and who will use it in the future?
- What are they looking for in the product?
- Have they expressed any particular void or unfulfilled need that your product could fill?
- What problems are they facing?
- What solutions are being offered in the market today that can resolve these problems?
- Why do you think a new product or a new release of your product is needed?
- How would your solution be different from existing ones?
- Why would your customers consider moving away from their current solutions?
- Is there a driving force or an emerging market trend that would suggest customers are ready to adopt your solution?
- What critical attributes should your product have to acquire early adopters and laggers?
- Which attributes would serve as key differentiators from other market offerings?
- What's the value proposition of your product?
- How could you both reduce the risks inherent to the market and improve your product's chance to succeed in the marketplace?
- And, how would this product benefit your company?

Yes, there are many questions to reflect on, even before crafting a robust and sustainable product vision! But, don't you worry, we are going to take things *"one small step"* at a time so that you can achieve this giant leap!

3.2.1 Define your Business Model

You can leverage the Business Model Canvas, a template designed to give you a quick, simple and single-page structure to develop your business plan. The FAQ: What is the Business Model Canvas? (Page 119) guides you in the use of this template through its nine building blocks. These building blocks articulate the who, the why, the what, and the how.

If you're a product owner in a small Start-up company, you're lucky! You can take the time (while avoiding the analysis paralysis) to be creative in developing each block of your canvas. And, if you're a product owner in a large and well-established company, well, you're lucky too! Different lucky but still lucky as you most likely don't need to worry much about the channels, the cost structures and revenue streams building blocks of your canvas – your company has quite likely already define best practices you can simply leverage and apply to your specific product.

With your Business Model Canvas completed, you should now have defined the value propositions of the product or service you want to create. You should also know how to reach your customer segments, and how to most efficiently deliver your offering.

This is a great starting point for you! The next step is to figure out how to best articulate your value propositions to your existing and prospective customers. This *articulation* should reflect your product vision and its values, as to avoid misinterpretation and focus on the delivered experience, while communicating and motivating your targeted customer segments to purchase your product or service.

3.2.2 Articulate the Problem Statement

Before drafting various candidate product vision statements, it always helps to put your thoughts on paper, to think about the actual problem to address, and create *"a concise description of the issue to be resolved"*. This is your Problem Statement. The more precise and complete you can be, the better.

Don't know where to start? Feeling overwhelmed? No problem! To make your life easier, and avoid the blank page syndrome, here is a simple method that will help you articulating the problem statement. Use the following format:

- Ideal: Describe the desired end-state
- Reality: Explain the concrete and actual situation at the present time
- Issue: Highlight the gaps between the current state and desired state
- Proposal: Layout an alternative solution to address the issue or exploit the missed opportunity

Here is an example:

> [Ideal] Customers should be able to use bitcoins to purchase groceries and shop in Brick and Mortar stores. [Reality] However, only traditional payment instruments, such as cash, check, electronic benefit transfer, debit or credit cards are available to them for making purchases in drugstores and shopping centers. [Issue] Payment through digital cryptocurrencies should be available to customers. [Proposal] The stores' Point-Of-Sale (POS) solutions could be enhanced to integrate cryptocurrency and digital currency exchanges as valid payment instruments.

The methodology to define this statement is discussed further in the FAQ: What is Design Thinking? (Phase 2: Define, page 133).

I must emphasize again that the problem statement should answer, clearly, concisely, and with no ambiguity, the 5 w's - who, what, where, when, and why.

3.2.3   Ideate Product Vision Statements

The basic rules in formulating a Problem Statement also apply here. A product vision statement must be clear and concise. It should also be stable enough to withstand external changes and time. It should be engaging, inspiring, and foster and generate the sustained need to purchase the product or acquire the service.

As described earlier, there is no certain and unique method to create and write a product vision statement. But, there are two commonly adopted formats; namely, Geoffrey Moore's, which is considered as more traditional, and Simon Sinek's, which takes the approach of communicating from the inside out. Regardless of the format you prefer, as the product owner, it is your responsibility to establish and define the product vision, and best communicate the message and value propositions of the product. Not an easy job! But, don't you worry, there's no reason to cry the wolf!

Indeed, there are methods available to the product owner to ideate various ideas that can take shape into product vision statements. One of these methods is briefly discussed in the FAQ: What is Design Thinking? (Phase 3: Ideate, page 134).

In the end, at this stage, the objective can't be simpler: let creativity flow.

3.2.4   Validate your Product Vision

You now have several candidate production vision statements. Some might be vague, too strong or too technical. Others might be way off-the-chart or too far-fetch for your specific market segment. In this final step, it's time to move from ideation to decision, and select the one statement that will best embodies and expresses the vision you have for the product.

To assist in the selection process, you may consider scheduling a few focus group meetings and inviting team members, existing or potential customers to provide you with raw and unfiltered feedback on the statements you came-up with in the previous step (Ideate Product Vision Statements).

Remember as well that a *good* Product Vision should:

(a) Be clear, simple and definite so as to avoid misinterpretation,
(b) Be sweet and short,
(c) Focus on the delivered experience,
(d) Align all activities, inputs, people, and factors involved in the product development process toward a unique goal, and
(e) Engage, inspire and motivate your target customer segment(s) to purchase the product.

Now you have a solid, robust and sustainable production vision statement. But, so what? What's next? What should you do you next?

As the product owner, you have two jobs, two tasks, namely:

1) Communicate: Your first job is to communicate your product vision to all product stakeholders, starting from the customers to the product sponsors and executives, via the product development teams. The more you communicate (or over-communicate) the product vision, the easier it'll be to transform your stakeholders into product ambassadors (and salespeople). All stakeholders need to comprehend and fully absorb the vision, whom the product services, why the product exists in the first place, what it does, and against whom the product may compete.

2) Dive Deeper: Your second task is to break this vision down into product themes, epics and user stories the product needs to comply with so that the vision can be actualized iteratively. It's also your responsibility as a product owner to ascertain the priority order in which these epics and stories should be delivered. Simply put, the next step is a game! It's all about definition and prioritization! So, let's play!

3.3   Determine the Product Themes

Through the implementation of a series of ideas, documented as User Stories, the product development team will eventually fulfill the production vision. What's a User Story? You may wonder.

As explained in the **Scrum Management**: *The Agile Practitioners Survival Guide*,

> ... A **User Story** is a statement which embraces a specific structure or template in order to present a need. Note that having a consistent template to document a User Story helps the Scrum team to understand better and faster the requirement.
>
> The most popular template, developed in 2001 by a team at Conextra, is: "As a `<role>`, I want `<goal/desire>` so that `<benefit>`." The "so that" clause is optional.
>
> With the introduction and adoption of the Persona concept, many Agile practitioners have opted to describe a User Story using the following format: "As `<persona>`, I want `<what?>` so that `<why?>`."

Considering all User Stories as equal and managing them the same way would be a mistake. Each story is different and, focuses on an identifiable and unique actor, role or persona. Each story captures a very particular need, a specific business, a functional, or a non-functional requirement. It's also important to understand that a user story may or may not stand on its own, and realize a minimal and viable deliverable; a user story – taken out of its end-to-end context- may provide absolutely no business value, but taken in a larger story may offer tremendous value.

In the **Scrum Management**: *The Agile Practitioners Survival Guide*, I explained the logical organization between Theme, Epic, User Story, Backlog Item, and Sprint Task. Below is a brief summary:

A **Theme** is a logical grouping of related User Stories. User Stories classified under the same theme should align with and contribute to a common goal. However, this goal cannot be achieved within a Sprint.

An **Epic** belongs to a particular Theme and documents a large unit of work that cannot be carried out during a Sprint. An Epic however, can be broken down into User Stories attainable within an iteration.

One key difference between an independent User Story, a User Story related to a Theme, and a User Story comprised in an Epic is that the latter does not accomplish its business value until the entire Epic is complete.

A **Backlog Item** represents a unit of work which is ideally small enough to be completed in one iteration. Epics and User Stories are Backlog Items.

A **Sprint Task** is not a Backlog Item and is not part of the Product Backlog. It's an activity that needs to be done so that a Backlog Item can be completed. In Scrum, a task is the smallest unit of work, which is classically estimated between four to sixteen hours.

Now that you have and understand what a user story, a theme, an epic, a backlog item and a sprint task are, and what they mean in the Scrum methodology, let's not waste any more time. Let's move into actions! And the first thing to do is to review the product vision, discuss the product high-level functional architecture, and start breaking it down into functional themes.

It's advisable to develop the product themes as a group, with the product development team, end-users, product sponsors and executives, etc. This exercise may seem daunting but, it's not that complicated. You just need a whiteboard to draw the product functional architecture. Then, review the Product Backlog and brainstorm with your team on how you would place each product backlog item into common and larger functional blocks. Still unclear? No problem! Let me explain further.

Let's consider the problem statement discussed in Articulate the Problem Statement on page 39. Assume your product vision statement is the following:

> "We believe in freedom. Enjoy life with no wall, frontier, and no hidden fee. Buy what you need, when you need it, wherever you live. The Freedom-Crypto Debit Card."

No need to be an expert in the banking industry to understand this example. Let us simply visualize the main functional components that are needed to build and offer a debit card to customers who own a cryptocurrency and digital currency exchange account.

First and foremost, you'll need a Customer Management functional component to (a) take care of the customer information, experience and interactions, (b) handle their orders or purchases, (c) manage any billing and revenue events, and (d) address quality and service level agreement problems. Second, you'll need a Partner (aka Engaged Party) Management functional component to (a) interface with traditional banking institutions and digital currency exchanges, (b) monitor and measure each partner's performance, as well as (c) manage any payment and settlement activities.

We could go on and on, but let's stop here. You got the idea. Let's however wrap-up by documenting the two discussed themes: (a) Customer Management Domain, and (b) Engaged Party Management Domain.

3.4 Determine the Product Epics

We reviewed what a theme is. We also used a simple technique to determine the main themes of your product, which consists in decomposing the product vision statement through the product functional architecture. We also defined what an Epic is, which is *a large unit of work that cannot be carried out during a Sprint*. So, let's not spend any more time defining the what, and dive straight into the how. And in particular: how do you determine product epics?

As the product owner, it's best if you know and master techniques that bring creativity out in the open: brainstorming sessions, focus groups, user group meetings, customer interviews, user stories refinement workshops, as well as indirect approaches such as questionnaires or online surveys.

And please, don't shy away from any of these techniques! Test them! Use them! Adapt them to your own needs, and remember that each has its own advantages and drawbacks, and will provide valuable insights into the development of Product Backlog.

Before diving into the development of product epics, collaborating with the product stakeholders, you should introduce the objective of the working session, and re-emphasize to all what the product vision statement is. You may as well ask the Scrum master to assist you in reviewing the current product state and Product Backlog. Bring along the solution architect or lead(s) and ask if they can go over the functional architecture so that all participants understand the overall picture. Then, take the lead, and re-center the team toward the specific functional area(s) you'd like to focus.

Experience suggests that it might be better to schedule four one-hour meetings, instead of conducting a lengthy and exhausting 4-hour working session during which you will ask the team to cover 4 product themes. Each one-hour meeting should focus on a single product theme. Why going for shorter meetings?

First, it'll be less challenging to find a 1-hour timeslot during which all key product stakeholders are available. And if you don't believe, try finding a 4-hour window where a handful of your critical product stakeholders are available. Give it a try, and you'll get the point.

Second, it'll be tough to keep all attendees focused one common goal during 4 long hours. It's just human nature. Everyone has its own responsibilities and often cannot afford suspending time for longer than a couple of hours.

Last, it'll make your job, as facilitator, way easier!

We won't discuss how to prepare for and facilitate a user story workshop at this point. This will be the topic of a later section. That said, you still need to understand what the expected outputs of such meeting are: (a) specific product personas should surface through the discussions, and (b) user stories (and in this particular case, the product epics) should be defined along with their respective acceptance criteria. Through this exercise, you may as well identify potential risks or opportunities you and your team may have to mitigate or exploit as you work together toward the realization of named product epics.

Let's go back to our example, the `Freedom-Crypto Debit Card`, and narrow our deep-dive in the `Customer Management Domain` product theme. This theme focuses on how individuals or organizations can obtain the product, how the customer information, relationship and interactions with the product are managed, and how the enterprise manages customer bills, collection of payment, overdue accounts, as well as handle billing events and any adjustments requests. On top of all of these, this product theme covers the overall customer experience throughout the product lifespan.

For now however, we will limit our discussion on how people can use a `Freedom-Crypto Debit Card (FCDC)`, and come-up with a few stories:

(1) As a `FCDC holder`, I want to `withdraw cash from an ATM (selling available bitcoins)` so that I `can purchase items at any stores.`

(2) **As a** FCDC holder, **I want to** deposit cash into my account at any ATM **so that** I can purchase additional bitcoins.

(3) **As a** FCDC holder, **I want to** use my debit card at any stores **so that** I can purchase grocery or other items.

(4) **As a** FCDC holder, **I want to** make online purchases using my debit card **so that** I can benefit from online product offerings and special deals.

(5) **As a** FCDC holder, **I want to** make online deposits into my account **so that** I can purchase additional bitcoins.

No need to go on; you get the concept! These user stories describe broad functionalities, and Product Epics are just that – large and complex user stories that cannot be designed, developed, validated and delivered within a two-week or monthly iteration. As any other user stories, an epic describes a person (or persona) fulfilling a specific task for a very particular reason. And let's not forget that an epic should also have clear acceptance criteria.

For example, let's use the epic (1) above on page 47. The acceptance criteria can be as follows:

1. The FCDC holder has a cryptocurrency or digital exchange account.

2. The total value available in the digital exchange account is greater than the amount to be withdrawn.

3. The FCDC holder has swiped and entered a valid PIN.

4. The requested amount and withdrawal fees were debited from the account.

5. The ATM has dispensed the requested cash amount to the FCDC holder.

6. The FCDC holder has received an email with the detailed transactions.

If you still have questions on how to determine and write your product epics, keep in mind that the methodology is exactly the same as the one used to define and write a user story. This process is discussed at great length in the FAQ: How to Write a User Story? (Page 142).

Lastly, once you're done developing your product epics, you'll still have plenty of time and opportunities to work with the team to further dive into the covered functionality and break it down into smaller and detailed user stories that can be developed and delivered within an iteration. That said, before you do, I'd suggest that you, as the product owner, spend a little bit of time to find out and understand better who your end-users and customers are, and develop the product personas...

3.5   Develop the Product Personas

A persona is a fictional character representing a user type. A persona leverages the product to achieve a very specific goal. The persona is typically developed with a real user in mind.

When developing a product persona, as the product owner, you should capture and analyze actual customer data so that the persona best model real-life end-users – and don't hesitate to give your persona a face! The more you personalize the product persona, the better you'll be able to prioritize the Product Backlog, the better the product development team will be able to understand the persona's specific needs, the better you will be positioned to build and deliver the right solution for your customers.

And, to do so, ask yourself the following questions: How old is your persona? What's its gender? What's its job? What's its income? What is the persona's problem or opportunity? What are its goals? How would the persona accomplish its goal with your product? What would the persona do without the product? Where would the persona use the product? What are the persona's main reasons for using the product? Is the persona tech-savvy? Is the persona a desktop or mobile user? How does the persona feel when using the product? Why does the persona specifically use the product?

Do a brief online search, and you'll find many examples and available templates to develop and document product personas. So, don't feel obligated or constrained in using the examples below. We all have preferences; techniques, methods or tools we'd feel more comfortable with. So, pick what makes senses to you. Pick what works best for you, and your specific needs, domain and product. But, always keep an open-mind to learn and add new tools into your toolbox.

Going back to our example, the Freedom-Crypto Debit Card, let's think about who could own and use such debit card, who could be a FCDC holder, the people in the product epics developed earlier in the section Determine the Product Epics (page 46). Could there be more than one user type? Obviously!

In our specific case, we can easily craft three different personas who would be interested in owning and using the infamous FCDC!

- **The retired couple:** Patrick and Lenah have been married for 30 years. Patrick is retired and Lenah will soon be. They invested in cryptocurrency several years ago. They decided to acquire a Freedom-Crypto Debit Card to limit their future 401k annual distribution, thus minimizing federal and state taxes, while maintaining their current lifestyle.

- **The young professional:** Yin has recently purchased a few bitcoins but has rapidly change his mind due to the market high volatility. He got a Freedom-Crypto Debit Card to slowly get rid of his digital assets while still hoping for the market to settle down and become bullish again.

- **The road warrior:** Malika has been day-trading and investing in digital currencies for several years. She loves traveling and exploring new countries. But she also wants to minimize the steep banking and currency exchanges fees that typically rhyme with traveling abroad. She obtained a Freedom-Crypto Debit Card specifically to make purchases during her travels and stop worrying about any hidden fees.

		Persona's Details	Persona's Goals
The Retired Couple	Patrick and Lenah	• Patrick is 64 years old, Lenah 62. • They've been married for 30 years and have 2 children and 1 grand-daughter. • Patrick worked for 26 years for the same company and retired 2 years ago. • Lenah is currently employed but plans on retiring in 2 months. • They invested in cryptocurrency 5 years ago to diversify their portfolio.	• They want to use their cryptocurrency assets to make daily purchases and minimize their 401k annual distribution.
The Young Professional	Yin	• Yin is 27 years old. • He graduated 3 years ago with a BA in Business Administration Management. • He works for a leading consulting firm. • He actively follows the financial news and decided to purchase five bitcoins.	• Yin no longer believes in bitcoins because of today's market volatility. He wants to slowly liquidate his assets while still hoping the market improves.
The Road Warrior	Malika	• Malika is 41 years old. • She works part-time as a Pharmacist. • She's been day-trading and investing in digital currencies for 10 years. • She frequently travels internationally to explore different scenery, culture, and cuisine.	• Malika wants to avoid currency exchange and banking fees while traveling.

FIGURE 3: PERSONA CARD EXAMPLES

Thus far, we discussed topics around the product ideation – the product vision, the product themes and epics – and did our best to define who the end-users exactly are. Before diving further into the product requirements with its short-term and long-term roadmaps, let's take a small break. Let's focus on how the people, the product owner in particular, can be most effective and efficient in collaborating with another key participant and pivotal role in the Scrum methodology: The Scrum master.

3.6   Work with the Scrum Master

Understanding your role and responsibilities as the product owner is not enough. You need to have a good grasp on who does what within the Scrum framework, and more specifically, you should appreciate the role and responsibilities of the Scrum master. Why? Because this knowledge will help you stay within the boundaries defined for your role, and best work and collaborate the Scrum master to achieve the team's final objective: the product release!

You're accountable for the delivered product, its quality and its return on investment. The Scrum master is the guardian of Scrum processes, the de-facto Scrum coach and facilitator, and the person responsible to ensure the Scrum teams continuously learn and improve its throughput.

On that note, let's figure out what it means for the product owner to work with the Scrum master starting with the Scrum ceremonies:

- **Backlog Grooming:** Since only the solution leads are typically in attendance, you're the one assigned to facilitate the ceremony. However, when only a handful of items need to be groomed, you might want to be efficient and combine both grooming and t-shirt size estimations. In this scenario, you'd be inviting the Scrum master and the team. You'd lead the grooming discussions, and let the Scrum master facilitate the estimation exercises.

- **Sprint Planning (part 1):** During this ceremony, you represent the customers, you're the Voice of the Customer. You clarify the business priorities and ensures all understand in the same way the relevant user stories. You're also the one recommending the sprint goal, which you prepared beforehand. On the other hand, the Scrum master is here to facilitate the ceremony, coach and ask probing questions to the participants (including you) so that the meeting's objectives can be obtained.

- **Sprint Kick-Off (or Sprint Planning Part 2):** Once there is no outstanding question on the user stories targeted for the next Sprint, you leave the room, but remain available if the team needs you. The Scrum master assists the Scrum team in breaking down the requirements into Sprint tasks, estimating the level of effort in hours, and committing to an achievable Sprint Backlog. At the end of the meeting, you can rejoin the room to review (and discuss) the committed scope.

- **Daily Scrum:** You listen; i.e.: it's not your meeting! It's the team's. Keep your lane, and let the Scrum master facilitate. Because this ceremony is a tactical one, and time is of the essence, the Scrum master ensures no lengthy design or requirements discussions take place during the meeting. In this case, the Scrum master invites the affected team members to *take it offline* and resolve the matter outside the meeting.

- **Sprint Review:** You start by going over the original sprint goal and Sprint Backlog. You then discuss the delivered product increments. The Scrum master facilitates the meeting, observes the attendees to mine any potential concerns. The Scrum master probes all participants to identify any potential concerns, and encourage them to raise any questions. You help clarify existing requirements and change requests as they surface during the meeting.

- **Sprint Retrospective:** The Scrum master runs the meeting and contributes too. You're an active attendee. Your role is to listen, discuss with an open-mind, and weigh-in on any inputs and learnings on the processes you own: Requirements Gathering, Backlog Grooming, Sprint Planning, etc. Work with and help the team assess if any changes are to be made. The Scrum master should assist the participants to feel comfortable enough to address all the topics. The Scrum master is also responsible to follow-up on the action items and improvements recommended during the meeting.

The collaboration between the product owner and the Scrum master doesn't end here. There are more than just meetings in our work day, right?

There is the **product**! You and the Scrum master should work together to build and deliver the product vision. While you're responsible and accountable to set and communicate the vision and the immediate priorities (i.e.: define the order of user stories must be built and released), you must rely on the Scrum master to achieve this vision.

In fact, the Scrum master should be your first ally! The Scrum master indeed ensures that the Scrum team embraces the vision and adheres to the current priorities. At the same time, the Scrum master reminds you that Rome wasn't built in a day, and helps you being realistic in your expectations. You can't get everything done in one Sprint! You need to account for the team's capacity!

There is the **Scrum team**! Unique individuals who collaborate and work together to achieve a particular goal. Because the Scrum master engages directly and daily with the team, the Scrum master has the necessary insights into the team members – sensing their emotional ups and downs, feeling their morale, acknowledging their challenges, and celebrating their successes. The Scrum master therefore continuously motivates the team.

You also have a pivotal role to play in keeping the team morale and productivity as high as possible. You must communicate (over-communicate!) the product vision and the reasons why a particular user story is so important.

Do try your best to be available when the team needs your inputs. Be open to discuss any issues and recommendations the team brings forward. Work with the Scrum master to escalate issues to higher-level stakeholders and executives, and resolve impediments the team faces.

3.7 Manage the Product Backlog

Let's start with the basis:

> The **Product Backlog** is a living list of ordered requirements based on added business value, risks, return on investment, etc. These requirements, captured as user stories (if possible), are called Product Backlog Items (or Backlog Items), and are typically new product feature requests, functional needs, non-functional constraints, bug fixes, existing functionality deprecation request, and so forth.

If the product owner would have one single task to excel in, it'd have to be managing the Product Backlog. The Product Backlog is indeed the beating heart of product to be built and delivered. And the sole owner of Product Backlog is you, the product owner! Yep! All is good. All is fine. But, in plain English, exactly, what does it mean to manage the Product Backlog?

The Product Backlog management includes
- (a) Collecting the product requirements,
- (b) Clarifying and refining the submitted backlog items and user stories,
- (c) Triaging the submitted backlog items,
- (d) Grooming the Product Backlog,
- (e) Setting a clear priority for each approved backlog items, and
- (f) Ensuring the development teams understand and work on the right user stories.

In the next sections, we'll elaborate on all of these pivotal activities.

3.7.1   Collect the Product Requirements

As the product owner, you spend your time analyzing the market trends, sensing any changes in direction, and reviewing potential regulatory mandates that may affect your existing product direction and long-term strategy. You are also in constant communication with your end-users, customers, project managers, development teams. You are therefore ideally positioned to collect new requirements, project change requests, and product enhancements from internal and external product stakeholders. And all of these requirements, you capture them in the Product Backlog!

Gathering requirements for the product to build isn't the sole responsibility of the product owner. All product stakeholders – from the end-user to the quality engineer – can add requirements to the Product Backlog. However, in the end, the product owner remains the accountable person for the completeness and quality of Product Backlog. In short, collecting requirements is only the first step in the process; and it's, perhaps, the easiest one!

3.7.2   Assist in the User Stories refinement

Once a requirement has been added to the Product Backlog, you should no longer call it a requirement. In Agile, requirements are product backlog items... And lucky you, as the product owner, you're typically the first one to review the recently added backlog items. Since not all product stakeholders are familiar with the peculiar format used in the Scrum methodology to document the product requirements, you often need to close the loop with the submitter to refine the added requirement so that it can be easily understood and acted on by the product team.

There are several techniques you can leverage to review a recently added product backlog item. Is the requirement SMART[2]? Does the added

---

[2] A SMART requirement is Specific, Measurable, Achievable, Relevant, and Time-Bound. For more information, refer to page 60 for the FAQ: What is a SMART Requirement?

backlog item meet all the INVEST[3] checks? Is the description clear? Can the description lead to confusion or open to interpretation? Are the business impacts or expected added value correctly documented? Does the backlog item include acceptance criteria?

To assist the submitter or any other product stakeholders in documenting their requirements in the expected format, you can typically count on the Scrum master to coach them in writing their requirements as user stories. But, you'll also spend a lot of time sitting with the submitter to refine their stories. So, for additional information, refer to the FAQ: How to Write a User Story? (Page 142).

3.7.3   Triage the Submitted Backlog Item

When product stakeholders add a user story in the Product Backlog, and work with you - the product owner – and/or the Scrum master to refine the added requirement, there is no guarantee that the request will actually be met. It's up to you to decide if the added user story is consistent and fits with the overall product vision, product roadmap and long-term business and product strategies.

You should also ensure that the requirement doesn't conflict an already approved backlog item or that it doesn't duplicate another. And, as you review the added requirement, keep the basic elements of a good backlog item in mind: Independent, Negotiable, Valuable, Estimable, Small and Testable. Then, decide! Approve or reject it. But, always inform the submitter of your decision!

---

[3] INVEST stands for Independent, Negotiable, Valuable, Estimable, Small, and Testable. You can read the detailed information on page 63: What is a Good Backlog Item?

3.7.4   Groom the Product Backlog

In the **Scrum Management**: *The Agile Practitioners Survival Guide*, I discussed at length what the Backlog Grooming ceremony consists of, and described its objective, frequency, duration, inputs, resources, attendees, agenda and outputs. So, to make a long story short, as the product owner, your goal in preparing, leading and facilitating the Backlog Grooming ceremony is to make sure the Product Backlog reflects accurately and timely the evolving business priorities.

For the product owner, this translates into the following three short-term goals:
- Ensure each backlog item has a clear acceptance criterion
- Prioritize the Product Backlog by placing the most important backlog items at the top and moving down the non-important ones at the bottom of the list
- Break down as needed the most important backlog items into smaller ones so that they can be assigned and completed within an iteration

Setting aside your short-term goals, your longer-term objectives are to prepare the Product Backlog for the upcoming Release and Sprint Planning ceremonies, and reduce as much as possible the elapsed time from the ideation of a User Story and its implementation.

3.7.5   Prioritize the Product Backlog

Prioritizing a list of requirements is not a novel thing! It's just common sense! And, as the product owner, it's your responsibility to define a clear direction for the product, and guide the product development team to build and deliver the most important or critical user stories first. But what user stories are truly important? Remember that if everything is important, then nothing is. So, let me repeat: what's important? What user story should be delivered first to the customers?

Marketing trends and evolving needs, external environment, insights into applicable regulatory entities, recently acquired information from competitors, rapid changes in customer needs, project milestones, expected business impacts of product backlog items to be delivered – all of these are essential inputs to prioritize the Product Backlog. And, the product owner is the sole product stakeholder accountable to ascertain and decide which user stories should be tackled and delivered now, which ones can wait for a few Sprints or the next release, or which ones can be worked on in the undefined future.

To successfully prioritize the Product Backlog, the product owner should understand all backlog items and in particular the business reasons behind each one. Typically, should there any doubts or questions on any backlog items, the product owner would discuss and clarify the requirement with the person who submitted the requirement. S/he would then reach out to and engage with, if necessary, the different levels of the organization – sales representatives, product managers, marketers, customers, end-users, and even C-level executives – to get their feedback. The product owner should then talk to project managers to get a grasp on any internal or external business risks, dependencies and impacts of these backlog items. And, needless to say, the product owner should talk to the Scrum team to identify any potential technical risks and unknowns that can affect the product release.

The product owner can stack-rank the product backlog items by defining a unique priority for each of them. But, in practice, you're better off using a simpler (and more efficient) technique such as the MoSCoW prioritization, where each product backlog item is classified as a Must Have, Should Have, Could Have, Wont' Have (at this time) requirement. See page 139 for the FAQ: What is the MoSCoW Prioritization?

In the end, the product owner should be able to assess the value proposition of each prioritized product backlog item and clearly articulate its value proposition both qualitatively and quantitatively. Once the list of submitted and approved user stories and backlog items have been prioritized, the items at the top of Product Backlog should provide the maximum business value, and, ideally, the maximum return on investment.

3.8 Define the Minimum Viable Product

At this stage, you have triaged, groomed and prioritized the Product Backlog. You should therefore have a fairly solid and comprehensive Product Backlog with all user stories ordered in the correct priority; the most important ones are detailed enough to be actionable and are placed at the top of Product Backlog as illustrated below.

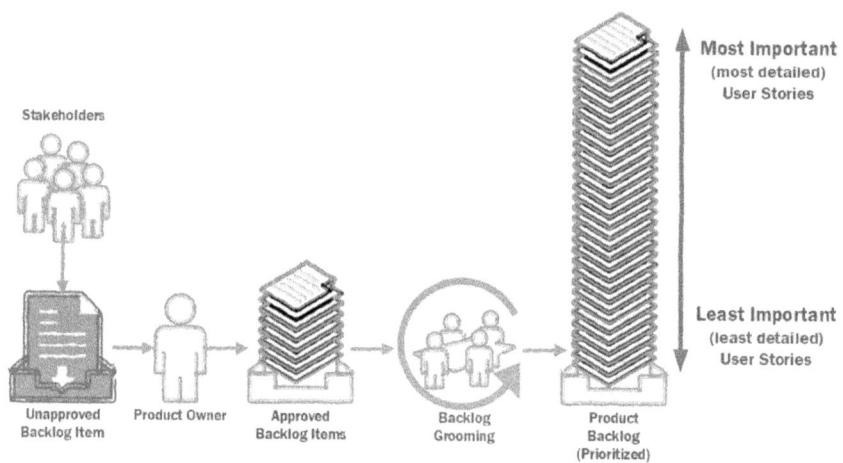

FIGURE 4: PRIORITIZED PRODUCT BACKLOG

All is great but, not surprisingly, that's not sufficient!

The product owner is typically the person who knows best the customer and understands its immediate needs. And, you ARE that person! No one else is responsible and accountable for building and bringing to market the right product, the Minimum Viable Product (MVP[4]). So, at the present time, your next logical step should be to determine what this MVP is. To do so, you can use one simple but critical input: the prioritized Product Backlog.

---

[4] Refer to page 67 for the FAQ: What is a Minimum Viable Product?

Developing the MVP consists of identifying the most important user stories that would provide enough value for people to use and purchase the product. These most important user stories are also referred as the Minimum Marketable Features or MMF.

The MVP and its associated features should capture sufficient interests from early adopters. The MVP should offer adequate benefits so early adapters become the de facto brand ambassadors of your product, participating, contributing, and better yet, leading marketing campaigns via social media and word-of-mouth. Thus, when defining your MVP, you should think about the methods that can empower these early adapters to provide feedback to the product development team and influence how features could or should evolve in future product releases.

In short, defining the MVP would assist you in scoping the next Product Release, and establishing the product roadmap.

3.9 Plan the Next Product Release (using User Story Mapping)

According to the Project Management Body of Knowledge (PMBOK® Sixth Edition), Agile Release Planning *"provides a high-level summary timeline of the release schedule (typically 3 to 6 months) based on the product roadmap and the Product Vision for the product's evolution. Agile release planning also determines the number of iterations or Sprints in the release, and allows the product owner and team to decide how much needs to be developed and how long it will take to have a releasable product based on business goals, dependencies, and impediments."*

In the **Scrum Management**: *The Agile Practitioners Survival Guide*, we detailed how to conduct the Release Planning ceremony and explained how it enables the product owner to get the Scrum team, product managers and stakeholders to agree and commit on a particular release plan. The release plan includes the scope and the timeline of next release (or increment) to build and deliver. And to make sure you have all the tools you need to be successful, I've extracted the related section from the Survival Guide and made it available as an FAQ: What is the Release Planning ceremony? (Page 153).

In this section, I'm not going to re-hash what I've already explained in the Survival Guide. Instead, I'm going to present a practical methodology for building the necessary bridge between the product themes, product epics, user stories and the product releases. And as you might have guessed based on the tile of the next section, this methodology is called: User Story Mapping!

3.9.1   Map your User Stories

Remember the `Freedom-Crypto Debit Card`? Great! Because we're going to apply user story mapping to plan the first release of our infamous debit card:

1. First, at the top of the page, list the product themes:
   a. `Customer Domain`
   b. `Engaged Party Domain`
2. Then, under each theme, list the associated product epics; For example, for the `Customer Domain` product theme, refer back to section Determine the Product Epics (page 46) for the associated product Epics
3. List the most important user stories for each product epic. For example:

   Product Epic: As a `FCDC holder`, I want to `withdraw cash from an ATM (selling available bitcoins)` so that I `can purchase items at any stores`

   a. **User Story #1:** As a `FCDC holder`, I want to `access USA Credit Unit's ATMs to withdraw cash from my available digital currency account(s).`
   b. **User Story #2:** As a `FCDC holder`, I want to `access any ATMs to withdraw cash from my available digital currency account(s).`
4. Think about the customer's journey and the absolutely required features the product must include so that it could acquire and attract a sufficient number of early adopters
5. Discuss each user story – and in particular, the Must Have and Should Have – and weigh-in the added-value of the user story
6. Review each user story with the team and product stakeholders. Discuss with passion, and probe and explore conflicting views. Think about the problem you're trying to solve, and always keep in mind the perspective of the customers
7. Agree on where to draw the line between user stories that will be included in the MVP and the ones that will be tackled later on, in future product releases

And here you have it! Your first User Story Map! Congrats!

	Customer Domain			
As a FCDC holder, I want to withdraw cash from an ATM (selling available bitcoins) so that I can purchase items at any stores.	As a FCDC holder, I want to deposit cash into my account at any ATM so that I purchase additional bitcoins.	As a FCDC holder, I want to use my debit card at any stores so that I can purchase grocery or other items.	As a FCDC holder, I want to make online purchases using my debit card so that I can benefit from online product offering and special deals.	As a FCDC holder, I want to deposit online payments into my account so that I purchase additional bitcoins.

Minimum Viable Product

As a FCDC holder, I want to access USA Credit Unit ATMs to withdraw cash from my available digital currency account(s).

Future Product Increments

As a FCDC holder, I want to access any ATMs to withdraw cash from my available digital currency account(s).	As a FCDC holder, I want to access USA Credit Unit ATMs to purchase additional digital currencies from cash.
	As a FCDC holder, I want to access any ATMs to purchase additional digital currencies from cash.

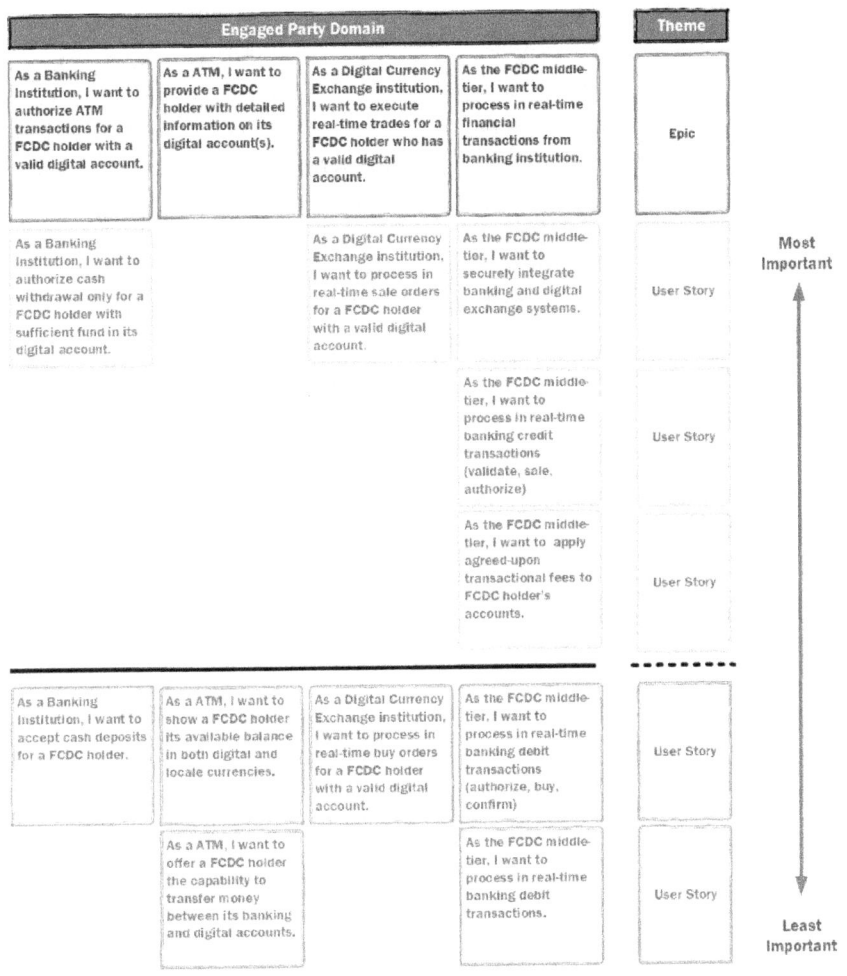

Engaged Party Domain				Theme	
As a Banking Institution, I want to authorize ATM transactions for a **FCDC** holder with a valid digital account.	As a ATM, I want to provide a **FCDC** holder with detailed information on its digital account(s).	As a Digital Currency Exchange institution, I want to execute real-time trades for a **FCDC** holder who has a valid digital account.	As the FCDC middle-tier, I want to process in real-time financial transactions from banking institution.	Epic	
As a Banking Institution, I want to authorize cash withdrawal only for a FCDC holder with sufficient fund in its digital account.		As a Digital Currency Exchange institution, I want to process in real-time sale orders for a FCDC holder with a valid digital account.	As the FCDC middle-tier, I want to securely integrate banking and digital exchange systems.	User Story	Most Important
			As the FCDC middle-tier, I want to process in real-time banking credit transactions (validate, sale, authorize)	User Story	
			As the FCDC middle-tier, I want to apply agreed-upon transactional fees to FCDC holder's accounts.	User Story	
As a Banking Institution, I want to accept cash deposits for a FCDC holder.	As a ATM, I want to show a FCDC holder its available balance in both digital and locale currencies.	As a Digital Currency Exchange institution, I want to process in real-time buy orders for a FCDC holder with a valid digital account.	As the FCDC middle-tier, I want to process in real-time banking debit transactions (authorize, buy, confirm)	User Story	
	As a ATM, I want to offer a FCDC holder the capability to transfer money between its banking and digital accounts.		As the FCDC middle-tier, I want to process in real-time banking debit transactions.	User Story	Least Important

FIGURE 5: USER-STORY MAPPING (EXAMPLE)

Isn't a dead simple visualization tool? But don't get fooled! Simplicity doesn't mean easy. But don't worry, creating this map is not your sole responsibility. All attendees of the Release Planning ceremony have a role to play in drafting this map. During the ceremony, emphasize the importance of getting it right to all product stakeholders. The map is a critical input in developing the Release backlog. Rely on the Scrum master to assist you in this process. But, remember that, as the product owner, you will always be the one held accountable for the next product release.

Last but not least, as you define the next MVP to be released, don't ignore the technical debt. The more you ignore an issue or postpone its resolution, the more complex and costlier it'll be for you and the product development teams to address. In plain English, if you can fix it today, don't wait for tomorrow. Better yet: *Do It Right the First Time!*

3.9.2   Consider the Technical Debt

Do it Right the First Time…

What an advice, right? After all it's just common sense. And, my sense tells me that if you pick up this book from the shelves, you most certainly don't need to be lectured about the cost of a defect and the cone of uncertainty concept. (See the FAQ: What is the Cone of Uncertainty? (Page 161).

That being said, as you define the scope of your next product release, try to convey the product sponsors and executives that the product must adhere to the highest quality standard possible to be relevant and have a chance to cross the chasm. It doesn't mean that you cannot ship a product that has defects: there is always one! But, it does imply that you have the ability to separate a critical defect impairing a key functionality of product from a minor problem. The first defect (the critical one) must be resolved before shipping the product, while the latter (the minor one) might be addressed in a future release. However, with this rationale, your technical debt will increase at each product release. And as the product evolves, it becomes more and more challenging to maintain the product and further extend its capabilities.

So, as you define your next product release, be always mindful that each release should ideally reduce your technical debt... Alright, enough said! Let's wrap-up and start drafting the release plan.

3.9.3   Develop the Release Plan

The Release Plan captures the purpose of the release, its scope and schedule, as well as its development, integration and testing strategies. It lists the assumptions, constraints, known risks and opportunities for the planned release. The previous two sections aimed at developing the Release Backlog with (a) the list of user stories that must be delivered to form the next Minimum Viable Product, and (b) the defects that must be resolved as part of the next release. The previous sections helped you define the release scope.

The next natural step is to build a delivery plan. This includes: (a) the story point estimates for each product backlog item in scope, (b) the teams and the number of resources (Scrum team members) that would be effectively working on the release. You can then calculate the number of Sprints required to consume and complete all the scoped release backlog items. Afterwards, you'll be leveraging both agile and traditional project management skillsets to:

- Develop a schedule
- Assess the risks to mitigate or avoid
- Document the opportunities to exploit or share
- Assign product backlog items to the teams who are best positioned to solve them
- Explain the methodology you'll use to manage the changes and
- Capture the approvals of release sponsors, such as executives and key stakeholders.

If it helps, you can take another cut at mapping your user stories by teams and Sprints. This view will assist you as well in the planning of upcoming Sprints.

	Sprint M1	Sprint M2	Sprint M3
Freedom-Crypto Debit Card (FCDC) Product Development Scrum Team	As FCDC, I want to securely integrate banking and digital exchange systems.	As FCDC, I want to map a FC debit card with an DCE account	As FCDC, I want to submit to USCU a cash deposit request to a valid USCA account
	As FCDC, I want to enable secured submission of trade orders to DCE	As FCDC, I want to submit to DCE a sale orders for a valid DCE account	As FCDC, I want to validate a sale order to DCE and cash deposit from DCE to FCDC account
	As FCDC, I want to enable secured submission of banking instructions to USCU	As FCDC, I want to map a FC debit card with an USCU bank account	
Digital Currency Exchange Inc. (DCE) Product Development Scrum Team	As DCE, I want to enable secured reception of trade orders from FCDC	As DCE, I want to process in real-time sale orders for a FCDC holder with a valid digital account.	As DCE, I want to validate a sale order from FCDC and cash transfer to FCDC account
USA Credit Unit (USCU) Product Development Scrum Team	As DCE, I want to enable secured reception of banking instructions from FCDC		As USCA, I want to accept from FCDC a cash deposit in a valid USCA account

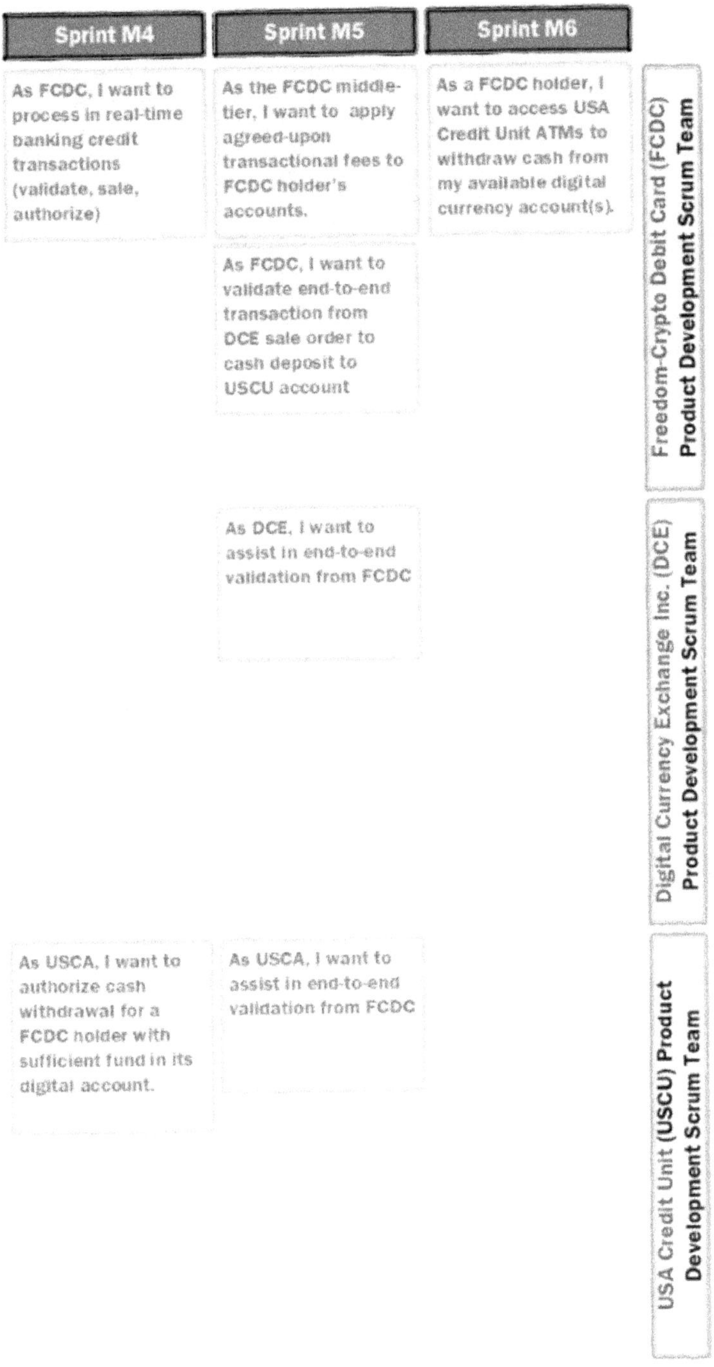

Sprint M4	Sprint M5	Sprint M6	
As FCDC, I want to process in real-time banking credit transactions (validate, sale, authorize)	As the FCDC middle-tier, I want to apply agreed-upon transactional fees to FCDC holder's accounts.	As a FCDC holder, I want to access USA Credit Unit ATMs to withdraw cash from my available digital currency account(s).	**Freedom-Crypto Debit Card (FCDC) Product Development Scrum Team**
	As FCDC, I want to validate end-to-end transaction from DCE sale order to cash deposit to USCU account		
	As DCE, I want to assist in end-to-end validation from FCDC		**Digital Currency Exchange Inc. (DCE) Product Development Scrum Team**
As USCA, I want to authorize cash withdrawal for a FCDC holder with sufficient fund in its digital account.	As USCA, I want to assist in end-to-end validation from FCDC		**USA Credit Unit (USCU) Product Development Scrum Team**

FIGURE 6: RELEASE USER STORY MAP BOARD (EXAMPLE)

And explained in the FAQ: What is the Release Planning ceremony? (Page 153), don't forget that the Release Plan is a living document you need to update at the end of each Sprint to reflect newly acquired information and latest progress made after completing the Sprint. It's an opportunity to adjust the Release plan and communicate bi-directionally the changes.

So, you now have a good handle on the next release to be delivered. But what's next? First, since you have a Release plan, as the product owner, you need to start planning the upcoming sprints. Second, you can start looking further down the road, working closely with product managers and stakeholders to figure out how to continuously increase the product value propositions and ascertain which user stories should be included in future releases, and acquire more customers as a result. And, you can assist the product managers in establishing the product roadmap...

3.10 Assist in Establishing the Product Roadmap

The product managers own the Product Roadmap, and since the product owner may or may not be the product manager, it is important to acknowledge, understand and recognize the responsibilities of both roles in establishing the product roadmap. While the product manager is technically leading the product roadmap, it's typical for the product owner to be the *active* and primary author of the roadmap document.

That being said, how do you start defining the product roadmap? Well, first you know what's to come: the next product release.

3.10.1 Establish the Short to Mid-term Product Roadmap

Begin with the User Story map created earlier (see Figure 6: Release User Story Map Board (Example) on page 69), and start laying out user stories and epics using time as scale.

This reorientation of the User Story map would help you visualize what your product roadmap could be; *"could"* because a product roadmap is much more than that. The product roadmap is indeed a flexible plan that lays out the short-term (3 to 6 months), mid-term (6 months to 2 years) and long-term (3 to 5 years) product goals.

While your immediate goals are clearly known and well-established (i.e.: you already know what the next product release is), your long-term goals are *certainly* fuzzier. Why *certainly*? Because no one can predict what the next 3 to 5 years have in store. The only circumstance where your long-term goals and product direction will be as clear as your short-term ones, is when the customer segment your product serves, is never affected by internal or external factors. And typically, this never happens! Change is part of life. Accept it. Embrace it. Because, in the end, you can't control all the variables. Uncertainties and unknowns are things we learn to live with.

So, as you work with the product managers to develop the roadmap, focus first on the short-term and mid-term goals. The short-term goals are known and defined by the MVP to build and deliver next. You can then prioritize the remaining of product backlog, sort the epics that will be adding the most value to the product in the next year or two, and map the user stories to one or two future releases as we did in Figure 7: User-Story Mapping Through Time (Example) (page 73).

Rely on the product managers who have the domain knowledge and understand the current and near-term market conditions and industry trends. Count on the solution architects with their expertise on todays and emerging technologies that would be suitable for the product. Of course, there is always a probability that the information you have and the assumptions you are making may not stand or be relevant in a year or so. This is why the product roadmap is just a tool to visualize what the product could become in the next few months.

Now, as far as the long-term goals are concerned, don't waste time arguing among yourselves about what the customers and the market would exactly be asking three to five years down the road. Instead, once a year, invite the product managers, solution architects, engineering leads, sponsors, executives, and key product stakeholders to meet face-to-face and conduct Scenario Planning workshops…

Release 1

Customer Domain

As a FCDC holder, I want to withdraw cash from an ATM (selling available bitcoins) so that I can purchase items at any stores.

As a FCDC holder, I want to access USA Credit Unit ATMs to withdraw cash from my available digital currency account(s).

As a FCDC holder, I want to deposit cash into my account at any ATM so that I purchase additional bitcoins.

Engaged Party Domain

As a Banking Institution, I want to authorize ATM transactions for a FCDC holder with a valid digital account.

As a Banking Institution, I want to authorize cash withdrawal only for a FCDC holder with sufficient fund in its digital account.

As a ATM, I want to provide a FCDC holder with detailed information on its digital account(s).

As a Digital Currency Exchange institution, I want to execute real-time trades for a FCDC holder who has a valid digital account.

As a Digital Currency Exchange institution, I want to process in real-time sale orders for a FCDC holder with a valid digital account.

As the FCDC middle-tier, I want to process in real-time financial transactions from banking institution.

As the FCDC middle-tier, I want to securely integrate banking and digital exchange systems.

As the FCDC middle-tier, I want to process in real-time banking credit transactions (validate, sale, authorize)

As the FCDC middle-tier, I want to apply agreed-upon transactional fees to FCDC holder's accounts.

	Q3H1	Q4H1	Y2
	Release 2	**Release 3**	**Release N**

Customer Domain

As a FCDC holder, I want to withdraw cash from an ATM (selling available bitcoins) so that I can purchase items at any stores.		As a FCDC holder, I want to access any ATMs to withdraw cash from my available digital currency account(s).
As a FCDC holder, I want to deposit cash into my account at any ATM so that I purchase additional bitcoins.	As a FCDC holder, I want to access USA Credit Unit ATMs to purchase additional digital currencies from cash.	As a FCDC holder, I want to access any ATMs to purchase additional digital currencies from cash.

Engaged Party Domain

As a Banking Institution, I want to authorize ATM transactions for a FCDC holder with a valid digital account.	As a Banking Institution, I want to accept cash deposits for a FCDC holder.	
As a ATM, I want to provide a FCDC holder with detailed information on its digital account(s).	As a ATM, I want to show a FCDC holder its available balance in both digital and locale currencies.	As a ATM, I want to offer a FCDC holder the capability to transfer money between its banking and digital accounts.
As a Digital Currency Exchange institution, I want to execute real-time trades for a FCDC holder who has a valid digital account.	As a Digital Currency Exchange institution, I want to process in real-time buy orders for a FCDC holder with a valid digital account.	
As the FCDC middle-tier, I want to process in real-time financial transactions from banking institution.	As the FCDC middle-tier, I want to process in real-time banking debit transactions (authorize, buy, confirm)	

FIGURE 7: USER-STORY MAPPING THROUGH TIME (EXAMPLE)

3.10.2 Establish the Long-term Product Roadmap

What is this *Scenario Planning*? Good question! It's a *"what if"* strategic planning methodology to determine the best possible direction to take (along with the product features and user stories to build) under certain assumptions on what the future will be. It's about imagining possible futures and determining how the product should evolve to best address the unique needs of these possible futures. Scenario Planning typically starts with a research phase before the product stakeholders are be invited to attend and contribute to a series of workshops.

1. Conduct an Academic Research: In this pre-planning or preparatory phase, you're going to (a) determine the main driving forces of your unique environment, and (b) identify the internal and external factors that could influence and shape the future of these driving forces. To facilitate this phase, you may consider hiring a consulting firm to conduct a PEST[5] analysis and identify the opportunities, risks, threats, uncertainties, emerging trends and industry dynamics your peculiar business may face over the next three to five years. At this stage, your objective is simple; you want to come up with an exhaustive list (and detailed description) of various factors (trends, uncertainties and dynamics) that could alter your current assumptions on what the future holds.

Let's go back to our study case: new regulations around the use of digital currencies and policy changes on international currency exchanges could drastically affect either positively or negatively the foundational premises of `Freedom-Crypto Debit Card`. But what else? What global trends, uncertainties and environmental dynamics could affect our assumptions on the future?

---

[5] PEST stands for Political, Economic, Socio-Cultural and Technology. PEST is a management methodology to conduct a strategic analysis or do a market research to identify environmental factors influencing an organization's operations. It is a tool to understand market growth or decline, business position, potential and direction for operations.

Well, let's start by listing all global, local, or technological trends we can think of!

- Policies and Regulations:
  - Privacy over customer personal sensitive information
  - Privacy around customer financial transactions
  - Protection of biometric digital identities
  - Regulation of traditional banking institutions
  - International Regulation around cryptocurrency and digital currency exchanges
  - Country-specific bans on cryptocurrency exchanges
- Industry:
  - Rise or decline of cryptocurrencies
  - Adoption level of cryptocurrencies by traditional banking institutions
  - New entrants in payment processing and solutions
  - Rise or decline of peer-to-peer payments
  - Merger and Acquisition in the Banking and Tech industries
- Technology:
  - Adoption level of online and mobile banking services
  - Technology innovation supporting banking activities
  - Agreement on a Common Information and Data Exchange Model for the banking industry
  - Evolution and adoption of blockchain technology
  - Cybersecurity threat and attack on digital currency exchanges

Let's now go over what we do know and do not know about the driving forces that could affect the trends and dynamics of tomorrow's marketplace; and what we feel or do not feel about the uncertainties the future holds.

- Policies and Regulations:
  - Would new or revised policies attract or prevent new entrants?
  - Would regulations and policies be centrally enforced?

- o Would new or revised regulations reduce the number of cryptocurrency and digital currency holders?
- Industry:
  - o How many people will be using cryptocurrencies?
  - o How many traditional banks will adopt digital currencies?
  - o How many digital currencies will be created?
  - o How many digital currency exchanges will be developed and participate?
  - o Would new payment or retail use cases surface?
- Technology:
  - o Would multiple common information models (CIM) be defined?
  - o Would the different data exchange standards be interoperable?
  - o How would cybersecurity requirements further impact banking and digital currency exchange systems?
  - o Who would hold the digital wallets enabling electronic transactions?
  - o How would cloud-computing systems and storage solutions accelerate deployment of a product?
  - o Which technology stack will lower the overall solution cost of ownership?
  - o How fast would ATM and POS be able to integrate cryptocurrencies?
  - o Would all digital currency exchanges support real-time transactions?

Third, let's consider the dynamics that could influence both trends and uncertainties. Dynamics are events and processes someone can generate or implement to steer a particular trend toward a desired direction. Dynamics can also reduce or increase the impacts of an uncertainty.

- Policies and Regulations:
  - o Elect an influencer in the company board of directors
  - o Participate in public panels and legislative discussions
  - o Contribute to the digital currency standards
  - o Include regulators in key business decisions

- Industry:
  - Collaborate with traditional banks and credit units
  - Help banking and financial institutions to develop business cases so that they can integrate digital currencies in their product portfolio
  - Be acquired by a financial institution
  - Merge with a digital currency exchange
- Technology:
  - Acquire a start-up in payments processing
  - Understand cybersecurity technologies
  - Ramp-up on common information model and data exchange standards
  - Train on cloud-computing systems

Before moving forward to the next step, you should share the above lists to all people who will be attending the Scenario Planning workshops. It's indeed time for everyone to meet face-to-face and work as a team.

2. Inject some Practicality into your Assumptions: The first Scenario Planning workshop consists of reviewing and discussing the factors identified during the pre-planning phase. Ask the attendees if other market forces – trends, uncertainties and dynamics – should be considered and added to the list. Have them agree on a final list which will be used to define various scenarios. Take a break.

During the break, draw on a whiteboard a matrix with two axes: the vertical axis measures the impact on the product (low to high, negative to positive), and the horizontal axis measures the predictability and uncertainty for a change in driving the identified forces or factors. This gives you a quadrant with four scenarios. When you reconvene the workshop, split the attendees into four groups. Each group is assigned a quadrant with the goal of determining the measurable state of major driving forces. The next figure illustrates what a possible quadrant of scenarios could be for the Freedom-Crypto Debit Card.

Positive/High Impacts	
Stricter regulations are put in place around cryptocurrencies exchanges and payment instruments Some banks and financial institutions adopt digital currencies Use of cryptocurrencies is limited online retail and peer-to-peer payments. Cyber-Security and Cloud-Computing systems begin adopting blockchain technologies Limited number of new entrants in cryptocurrency payment instruments	Regulations support cryptocurrencies exchanges and payment instruments Banks and financial institutions adopt digital currencies Cryptocurrencies cross the chasm and become a new standard for retail and peer-to-peer payments. Cyber-Security and Cloud-Computing systems fully embrace blockchain technologies Limited number of new entrants in cryptocurrency payment instruments
Stricter regulations are put in place around cryptocurrencies exchanges and payment instruments Limited number of banks and financial institutions adopt digital currencies Use of cryptocurrencies is limited to peer-to-peer payments. Cyber-Security and Cloud Computing systems adopt some blockchain technologies Large number of new entrants in cryptocurrency payment instruments	Regulations make cryptocurrencies exchanges illegal Use of cryptocurrencies is marginalized Cyber-Security and Cloud-Computing systems don't embrace blockchain technologies
Negative/Low Impacts	

(Left axis label: Predictable; Right axis label: Uncertain)

FIGURE 8: SCENARIO PLANNING MATRIX (EXAMPLE)

3. Develop the Scenario Narratives: This third phase is typically conducted the next day. Reaching agreement on the four high-level scenarios can be challenging and, as the product owner, you'll have to leverage all your facilitator skills to keep the attendees focus on resolving the specific problems of each quadrant. And so, the next day, to kick-off the session, do a quick recap of previous day activities and accomplishments, and then go over the defined quadrant. Probe the attendees to validate their agreement and commitment. Afterwards, you'll split the attendees again into four groups.

Each group is assigned one specific scenario with the objective of developing a narrative around this scenario. Ideally, you'd have arranged a meeting room for each group so that attendees can work without distractions from the other groups. The scenario narrative should include all the assumptions made on the considered trends and uncertainties. It should also discuss the events that would lead to the future depicted in the named scenario. You should as well brainstorm and think about how you'd identify the precursors that would indicate this scenario is the one! For example, a cyberattack against a financial institution resulting in millions of stolen bitcoins would likely result in stricter cybersecurity policies and regulations applicable to the digital currency exchanges.

Give each group four hours to develop a narrative. If you've hired a couple of strategy consultants to help you conducting the scenario planning workshops, have them work with each group to answer any questions or concerns about the narrative. The more detailed and precise the scenario narratives are, the better prepared you'll be in dealing with what the future could hold, and orienting your product in the right direction.

Once the narratives are drafted, bring each group together and have them present their analysis. Invite the other groups to share their feedback, ask questions, or raise any concerns or doubts about the market forces and conditions driving this specific scenario. By doing so, you'd validate the trends, uncertainties and dynamics, which form the unique and specific foundation of each scenario.

4. Determine the Product Directions: At this point, you've completed the most difficult phases. But, you still have one more thing to figure out: how would you deal with each possible future you've just identified. Do you need to articulate your problem statement differently for each scenario? Is your current product vision sustainable? How should user stories be prioritized to best address each scenario? Or do you need to ideate new user stories to deliver a product that would add value to the customers in each of these alternative futures? In short, it's time to come-up with recommendations and construct a possible roadmap that address the requirements of each unique scenario you may face over the next 3 to 5 years.

Probability and uncertainties aside, the product roadmap remains a valuable tool to help the entire organization and product development teams agree on the next steps, understand the cost and benefits of building the product.

The product roadmap also helps all stakeholders to work better together in closing the gaps between the current and ideal state, and per se, to achieve the product vision.

That said, now that you know where the product is heading toward over the next few months and years, let's focus on today, and concentrate on the work we need to accomplish over the next couple of weeks.

Let's manage the Sprint!

3.11 Manage the Sprint

In Scrum, the product is designed, developed and validated through iterations, called Sprints. The duration of a Sprint is typically two to four weeks, but can extend to a month. Each Sprint gives you, as the product owner, the chance to build product increments that can be delivered in the next planned product release. It also enables you to get closer – one increment at a time – from the product vision. And, to achieve this desired outcome, the only thing you must do is to steer the boat in the right direction...

Managing the Sprint is to:
- (a) Define a concrete and specific goal for the Sprint,
- (b) Prepare the Sprint Planning ceremony,
- (c) Review and approve the Sprint Backlog (after the Sprint Kick-Off),
- (d) Shield and assist the Scrum team during the Sprint,
- (e) Represent the voice of the customer,
- (f) Evaluate the progress made during the Sprint,
- (g) Review the produced Potentially Shippable Product Increments, aka PSPI,
- (h) Learn from the completed Sprint, and
- (i) Do it all over again!

In the next sections, we're going to discuss and dive into each of these activities.

3.11.1 Define the Sprint Goal

As the product owner, you are responsible to set and define a concrete and specific goal for the forthcoming Sprint. This sprint goal will help the Scrum master and the Scrum team in planning and developing the Sprint Backlog during the Sprint Planning meeting. Since you've already planned the next product release in Develop the Release Plan (page 67), you should now have a good understanding on what the next few sprints should look like, as illustrated in the Figure 6: Release User Story Map Board (Example) (page 69). This is the advantage of planning a release using with the right tool; you can get way ahead of the curve, cool, right?

So, what is a sprint goal? According to the Scrum Guide, *"the sprint goal is an objective set for the Sprint that can be met through the implementation of Product Backlog. It provides guidance to the Development Team on why it is building the Increment."*

Three things must be made clear at this point. First, the goal is articulated in business terms only. Second, it answers a very simple question: why the team should even work during this Sprint. Third, the goal should motivate and be achievable as well as measurable so that the Scrum team can understand the reason why it has to work efficiently and effectively, and determine easily (visually ideally) at the end of the Sprint if the goal is reached.

For example, looking back at Figure 6: Release User Story Map Board (Example) (page 69), the goal of Sprint M1 and Sprint M2 are clear; Sprint M1 is about enabling the financial transactions between Freedom-Crypto Debit Card (FCDC), Digital Currency Exchange Inc. (DCE) and ATMs operated by USA Credit Unit (USCU). Sprint M2 is to submit a Sale Order to DCE so that a FCDC customer can withdraw cash at an ATM operated by USCU.

With a concrete and precise goal in mind for the upcoming Sprint, you can start preparing for it.

3.11.2 Prepare the Sprint

Let's begin with a simple definition:

> The **Sprint Backlog** is the committed list of user stories, backlog items, requirements and Sprint tasks the Scrum team plans on addressing during the Sprint. The list is developed from the Product Backlog (or Release Backlog) based on each item's priority and available information.

Leveraging the defined sprint goal, the product owner, the Scrum master, the solution leads, the Scrum teams, the project managers and, at times, other stakeholders meet and collaborate during the Sprint Planning (part 1) to determine what product features and user stories should be built and delivered at the end of the next Sprint.

The outcome is a tentative list of prioritized product backlog items to develop and deliver during the next Sprint. This list is not the final Sprint Backlog but, it's something the Scrum team can take forward to the Sprint Planning Part 2 (also known as the Sprint Kick-Off).

During this second ceremony, the Scrum team breaks down the what – the user stories, backlog items, defects, functional and non-functional requirements, etc. – into tasks, which defines the how. The Scrum team estimates each Sprint task and then commits to a specific scope of work as laid in the Sprint Backlog.

3.11.3 Review the Sprint Backlog

While the Scrum team is responsible and accountable for defining the Sprint Backlog, you are the ultimate accountable person for the product increments that will be delivered at the end of the Sprint. Hence, it's of prime importance that you take the necessary time to review the Sprint Backlog, and ensure the completeness of each committed backlog item. Ask yourself if the backlog items are Independent, Negotiable, Valuable, Estimable, Small and Testable. You can refer to the FAQ: What is a Good Backlog Item? (Page 141) for more information. You can also review the differences between the Product Backlog and a Sprint Backlog, referring to the named FAQ (page 151).

The good news is that you now have a list of committed user stories, backlog items, requirements and Sprint tasks the Scrum team will be focusing on and work hard to deliver within the next iteration. You'll soon have product increments to validate, product increments that could possibly be shipped in just a few days! But it can only happen if you assist in reducing any interferences that may jeopardize the commitment made by the team…

3.11.4 Shield the Scrum team during the Sprint

Once the Sprint is kicked-off, all the product stakeholders should have formed a clear (and the same) understanding of the anticipated product increments that will be delivered at the end of the Sprint. The Sprint Backlog captures this anticipation, the list of backlog items the Scrum team has committed to deliver during the Sprint.

Now, it's all about executing the plan. It's about being effective and efficient. It's about staying on course. While the Scrum master plays the main role in protecting the team from any interferences – including the interferences you (Yes! You, the product owner) may generate – you should do your best to also protect and shield the team during the Sprint. What does it mean for you?

First, after the Sprint kick-off, you should avoid requesting the team to accommodate and integrate an additional user story without agreeing on de-scoping another. If you do push the Scrum team to include a user story without removing any committed backlog items from the Sprint Backlog, you're likely to open a can of warms; the Scrum team may indeed be required to cut corners to complete all backlog items. And cutting corners typically ends-up with product increments that don't meet the expected quality standards, and in consequence, an increased technical debt. Not the greatest outcome! The complete opposite of what you actually desire.

Second, you need to inform and continuously educate the customers, your peers, and managers to submit their requests (new requirement, variance, question, change request, etc.) in the form of a User Story that is to be added to the Product Backlog. And as discussed in the section Manage the Product Backlog (page 55), before the team can work on these requests, you must first triage, groom and prioritize them so that they can be considered in the current or in a future Sprint. Having all the product stakeholders understand and comply with this process would reduce (a) the number of people inquiring, complaining, or asking for impromptu changes to one of your Scrum team members directly, and (b) non-urgent and non-important noise that can deviate the team from the work already committed and documented in the Sprint Backlog.

Last but not least, as the product owner, you naturally want each product increment (and the product release) to be delivered as soon as possible; after all, it makes business sense, doesn't it? The shortest time to market is what all sponsors, executives, and customers are asking in today's world. The sooner you get the product out of the door, the sooner your customers benefit from it, the sooner you get cash into the bank, and the sooner you start working on the next release to build and deliver.

But, there are two sides to every coin. If you don't protect the Scrum team to take the necessary time to ramp-up and train its new team members, you'll end up with a product development team on the verge of crashing into flame. Burned-out senior resources and untrained rookies (no offence intended). The entire team will end-up being demoralized, and unsurprisingly will be looking for a way out. So, be smart, protect the team against unsustainable work patterns. Accept small short-term delays, and trust the team to do the right thing not only for the current Sprint but for the future ones.

3.11.5 Represent the Voice of the Customer

By now, you should know my inclination to start with the basics. After all, before showing up at the start line of a marathon, we need to train, build up our cardio, and run a few miles, right? So, before delving into this peculiar duty of the product owner, let us define what the *Voice of the Customer* is.

According to Wikipedia, *"in business and Information Technology, the Voice of the customer (VOC) is used to describe the in-depth process of capturing customer's expectations, preferences and aversions. The Voice of the Customer is a market research technique that produces a detailed set of customer wants and needs, organized into a hierarchical structure, and then prioritized in terms of relative importance and satisfaction with current alternatives."*

Sounds familiar, yes? Because, it should sound very familiar! In Scrum, the VOC translates into a very central artifact: The Product Backlog! And since, as the product owner, you own the Product Backlog, you're logically the best person to understand the *"customer wants and needs"* and speak on their behalf.

Hence, during the Sprint, when the Scrum team has questions or doubts regarding a User Story, there should be minimal need to relay the questions to the customers or end-users. You should be able to answer and clarify the team's questions, and represent the Voice of the Customer. In the worst-case scenario, you can always coordinate and schedule a meeting with the customer so that the Scrum team can be unblocked as soon as possible.

3.11.6 Assist the Scrum team during the Sprint

Representing the Voice of the Customer is one obvious way to assist the Scrum team during the Sprint. But, there is much more the product owner can do to help the team achieve the sprint goal and grow to become a high-performing team.

First, know your role and responsibilities, accept the boundaries defined by the Scrum methodology, avoid micro-managing the team, and don't act as the Scrum master. Instead, do your best to collaborate and be a servant leader to both the team and the Scrum master.

Second; participate in the daily scrums. This is your chance to stay connected and informed of the progress made, as well inspect and fine-tune the product increments as they get built. So, grab and hold on to this opportunity. Remember however this ground rule: the meeting is for the Scrum team to self-organize to achieve the committed scope of work. You may attend the meeting but you're only attending as a listener! It's a tough rule, but, there are reasons behind it:

1) The meeting is intended for the Scrum team to discuss openly tasks and roadblocks

    You may think adding your two cents or providing feedback on a particular topic might help the team but, it could in fact have the opposite effect: a Scrum team member may decide not to speak up, ask a question to its peers, rise its concerns, or flag a roadblock.

2) People outside the Scrum team may not understand (or care about) the technical tasks

    Some stones are better left unturned. You're certainly the Voice of the Customer, control the Why, and have a say in the Customer Experience to deliver. But, the How is not your responsibility. So, let the team figure out the best solution to build and deliver the expected deliverable.

3) The Daily Scrum is not a vertical status reporting meeting

    As the team members explain what they did yesterday, what they plan on doing today, and what issue or roadblock they face, it's tempting to use this information to report on the current Sprint progress... Three words of wisdom for you: avoid the temptation!

Indeed, even though a team member might be stuck on a Sprint task, it doesn't mean the associated user story won't get done. Don't forget the Scrum team is self-organized and shares accountability. The team will work together on finding a path forward. If they can't and need assistance, they will escalate the issue, and the Scrum master will reach out to the right person (including you) to do the needful in assisting the team and removing any impediments.

Hence, the product owner (and the project manager) typically sends product release status reports (and project status reports) at the end of each Sprint.

4) The Daily Scrum is not a problem-solving session

    Putting aside technical problems that may surface while working on a Sprint task, a team member may have questions about a user story and what the customer experience should be. As the product owner, you'd likely want to step in right away and explain the requirement, diving into the end-to-end customer journey to deliver for the particular user story. Well, don't! Instead, simply inform the team that you are available right after the Daily Scrum to discuss and clarify the user story.

Third; be transparent! Owning the Product Backlog doesn't mean you should have full-control over it. You may be responsible and accountable for the Product Backlog but all internal product stakeholders should have easy access to it and be able to submit their own requirements and ideas. The Scrum team members often have good ideas for the product! Not allowing them to access the backlog, help in the product ideation, write and submit their own user stories would have detrimental effects on your team, the product, and your organization. Understood? Be transparent, and build a shared understanding of the product scope and vision.

Fourth; the product owner has a unique authoritative and de facto position to influence how the Scrum team can evolve and grow. Agreed, it's not your responsibilities to form a high-performing team. Nevertheless, you can always contribute positively to both the product and the team, killing two birds with one stone. How? Trust the process. Trust the people. You're not the only one who wants to build the product and makes it available to the largest number of customers. The Scrum master and the Scrum team have the same goal. They are also the ones who can best master the way the product should be built. So, give them credits for that!

Give them the necessary time as well to do it right, and do it right the first time. The team must have the skills to develop a solution addressing the customer needs. To acquire the required skills, the team must spend sufficient time to learn, continuously improve, and train on the emerging technologies. Of course, this may reduce the team's throughput for a couple of Sprints. This is fine! There is always an upfront fee to pay for being more effective and efficient. And, if you empower the Scrum team to self-organize for increasing both quality and productivity, the product sponsors and executives will follow your steps and do the same. Trust your team to do the right thing.

Last, while trusting your team is essential, it's not sufficient. To best assist the Scrum team, you should embrace, communicate and over-communicate the Scrum values to all product stakeholders, including the team! And don't be afraid to bring it up during the Sprint retrospective if you feel the team or group of individuals don't demonstrate or accept the Scrum values: respect, commitment, openness, focus and courage.

3.11.7 Evaluate the Sprint

Thus far, we cover activities relevant to the initiation (envisioning), planning (road-mapping) and execution (releasing) of a Sprint. But, that's not all. Don't forget that you're accountable for the product's return on investment: You must ensure that the Scrum team delivers the product increments within the available budget, and expected timeline. Scrum doesn't mean there are no deadlines and budget constraints to deal with. You therefore have the critical responsibility to monitor and control (adapt) the Sprint. Again, don't worry, you're not alone. You can rely on your new best friend – the Scrum master – to give you all the tools you need to ascertain the progress made, and figure out whether the planned activities are on track, if a drastic change might be required, or if the Sprint should be simply terminated!

Before diving into the two tools you'll be using intensively, namely the Sprint burndown chart and the Team Velocity, let's talk about termination. Strangely enough, the product owner has rarely the guts to make this difficult call and end a Sprint that is clearly going haywire.

3.11.7.1 Terminate the Sprint

The truth is that we all have experienced a Sprint that did not go as planned. We all have experienced a Sprint during which the number of impediments were so many, that we – the Scrum team, the Scrum master and the product owner – decided to drop half of the committed user stories from the Sprint Backlog, and add other requirements to use the available capacity (if any left). Why? Why not terminate the obviously unmanaged Sprint and restart from scratch? Because, we are all human! Termination is too often considered as a failure. It's not! Terminating a Sprint is not a failure! In certain conditions, it's the right and only logical choice to make! Imagine that! Yes! I am indeed telling you that terminating a Sprint can be the solution, can be the right call to make. Sounds crazy, doesn't it? Let me explain further.

Put yourself into the shoes of a corner-man. Your fighter is being outclassed and is clearly in danger, risking its health and life. Would you keep the fight going, knowing exactly how bad it's going to end? Would you wait for your fighter to be unconscious, lying face down on the mat? Or, would you throw the towel before it's too late? My guess is that you'd do the smart thing: you'd throw the towel. You'd protect your fighter, accept the loss, and work to make the necessary corrections for the next fight. Logical, right?

Well, terminating the Sprint is exactly the same! You recognize being on the wrong course – the team struggles because of an external dependency not being completed; an impediment is blocking progress on critical user stories; a business change is requiring the revision of current priorities, etc. Hence, to avoid wasting everybody's time and before the team gets frustrated and loses momentum, you'd logically ask the Scrum master to terminate the Sprint. Nothing wrong with that!

3.11.7.2 Review the Sprint Burndown Chart

In the **Scrum Management**: *The Agile Practitioners Survival Guide*, among other things, we explained what a burndown chart is:

> "A burndown chart is a graphical representation of work left to do versus time. The outstanding work (or backlog) is often on the vertical axis, with time along the horizontal. That is, it is a run chart of outstanding work. It is useful for predicting when all of the work will be completed" (Wikipedia).
>
> The Sprint burndown chart graphically represents the total work required to complete during the Sprint and displays the progress made by the Scrum team to reach the sprint goal. The X-axis represents days in the Sprint, while the Y-axis contains the effort remaining (usually in ideal engineering hours). This chart makes the work of the Scrum team visible to all, and is in fact the best available tool for the Scrum master, the product owner, and project managers to monitor and control the Sprint execution.

As the team works on the committed User Stories, and updates the status of each Backlog item and assigned Sprint task, the Sprint burndown chart should automatically reflect the progress made. The team is either behind, on track, or ahead of schedule. As the product owner, you must understand (a) how to quickly read such chart, and (b) what to do when things go way better than expected, are on track, or not. To help you in this particular task, I'm going to re-use the examples documented in the Survival Guide. Why the same examples? Because, even though there are more ways than one to skin a cat, sometimes, it's best not to change what isn't broken!

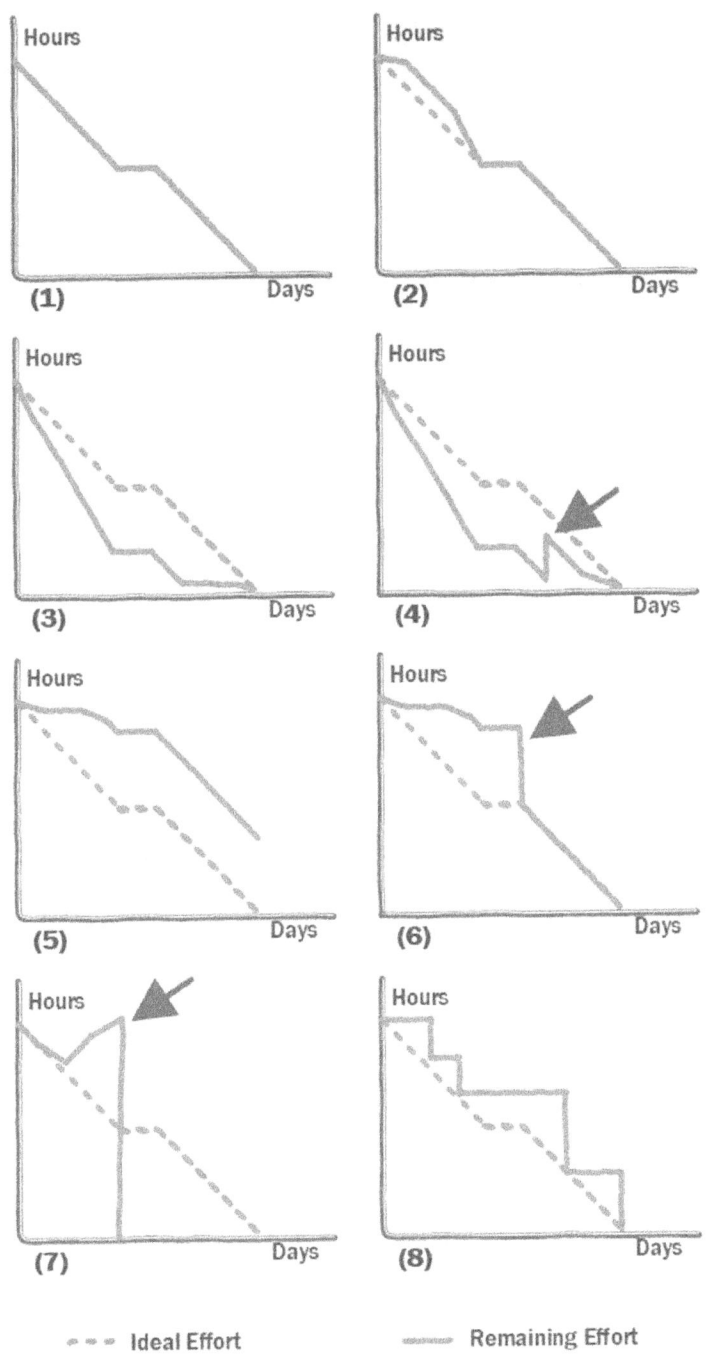

FIGURE 9: SPRINT BURNDOWN CHARTS

Interpretation of previous Sprint Burndown Charts:

(1) *The Scrum team executes perfectly the Sprint and achieves the sprint goal.*

You have an all-star team! Keep up the good work.

(2) *After a slow start, the Scrum team manages to get back on track, and achieves the sprint goal.*

Assuming each team member has updated daily its assigned Sprint tasks, you're a lucky product owner. Congratulate the team during the Sprint Review. During the Retrospective, understand if anything could have been improved in the Sprint Planning stage so that the observed slow start could be mitigated or avoided in future sprints. Take charge and ownership of your processes. And work with the Scrum master to capture the learnings, and adapt the Sprint Planning ceremony if need be.

(3) *The Scrum team resolves faster than expected the Backlog Items scheduled as part of the Sprint, and decides to get some rest at the end. The Scrum team does achieve the sprint goal.*

You had high hopes a few days into the Sprint. Wishful thinking! Something happens. During the Retrospective, don't shy away from asking the team the reasons why. Don't assume anything! One of the team members may have gone on vacation and the slowdown observed at the end of the iteration was actually expected. Maybe, the team had to attend a training during the second part of the Sprint and so decided to put extra-effort at the beginning to guarantee success. Or, the team lost motivation. Just ask, and work with the Scrum team to make the needed adjustments.

(4) *The Scrum team resolves faster than expected the Backlog Items, and decides to add new Backlog Items to the Sprint Backlog. The Scrum team exceeds the sprint goal.*

Wow! You're definitely a happy camper! The team manages to get more work done than anticipated. During the Retrospective, you should nevertheless ask if the team may have over-estimated the effort associated with the committed user stories. You indeed want to rule out any misunderstanding or process issues with the estimation techniques used by the team. Check with the Scrum master if a refresher on how to obtain definitive estimates[6] during the Sprint kick-off is needed.

(5) *The Scrum team experiences challenges resolving the committed Sprint Backlog. The Scrum team does not achieve the sprint goal.*

What went wrong? The team visibly struggles throughout the Sprint to complete the committed user stories. Has the team over-committed? Were there too many interruptions? Which impediments cause the most delay? Did the team raise any concerns during the Sprint? Was the Scrum master sufficiently engaged? Were you engaged? Did you make yourself available to assist the team? During the Retrospective, ask the attendees for inputs and recommendations to avoid similar situations in future Sprints. Follow-up with the Scrum master to make sure appropriate changes are made, and set aside additional time to better monitor the next Sprint, assist and encourage the team.

---

[6] A Definitive estimate is a bottom-up estimate and is the most accurate estimate the product development team can determine without completing and delivering the product increment. The range of variance between the Definitive estimate and the actual cost is relatively low: 10% more and 5% less.

For more information, you can refer to the FAQ: How do Estimates Evolve with the Product Development? (Page 4-46)

(6) *The Scrum team experiences challenges to complete the committed Sprint Backlog, and decides to remove some originally committed Backlog Items from the Sprint Backlog to partially achieve the sprint goal.*

Good news! The team is being proactive, and is not afraid of acting fast to avoid a total train wreck. This generally implies a certain level of maturity in your applied development processes. As the team makes the decision to drop the blocked backlog items from the Sprint Backlog, work with the Scrum master to perform a root cause analysis so that the removed backlog items can be considered in an upcoming Sprint.

(7) *The Scrum team experiences challenges to resolve the committed Sprint Backlog, and decides to terminate the Sprint earlier.*

The Sprint was clearly going haywire, and you made the difficult but necessary decision to terminate the Sprint. It's all good though! You didn't waste time. You recognize a major issue and stop. Failing fast is just another sign of maturity. You should however ask the Scrum master to schedule and conduct a Retrospective to learn from this little failure. Capture the learnings and apply them to future sprints. You and the team can then go back to the whiteboard and start planning the next Sprint.

(8) *The Scrum team seems to achieve the sprint goal but since the Scrum team doesn't update the Backlog Items being worked on regularly, the Sprint burndown chart is useless.*

You have a serious problem! Set aside some very much needed time with the Scrum master to make your expectations clear. The Scrum master and each team member should not only appreciate the need to update their assigned tasks daily, but understand the reasons why it's so critical. You should consider bringing a certified coach or an agile consultant to assist the team.

3.11.7.3 Review the Sprint Burnup Chart

An alternative to the Sprint burndown chart is the Sprint burnup chart. The burnup chart is a graphical representation of the amount of work that has been completed against the total amount of work to complete. The vertical axis shows the amount of work completed measured in number of tasks, estimated hours or story points, whichever you decided. The horizontal axis is time measured typically in days. Progress is then plotted as a line that grows up to meet a horizontal line representing the forecast scope.

One key advantage of using a burnup chart is that it enables you to easily visualize when the scope changes: The horizontal line representing the forecast scope goes up or down if scope is added or removed. For example, in the below figure, on Day 5, the team added a backlog item to the Sprint (the work progressing better than expected), but on Day 9, opted to de-scope it (an impediment may have surfaced and prevented the team to complete the added backlog item).

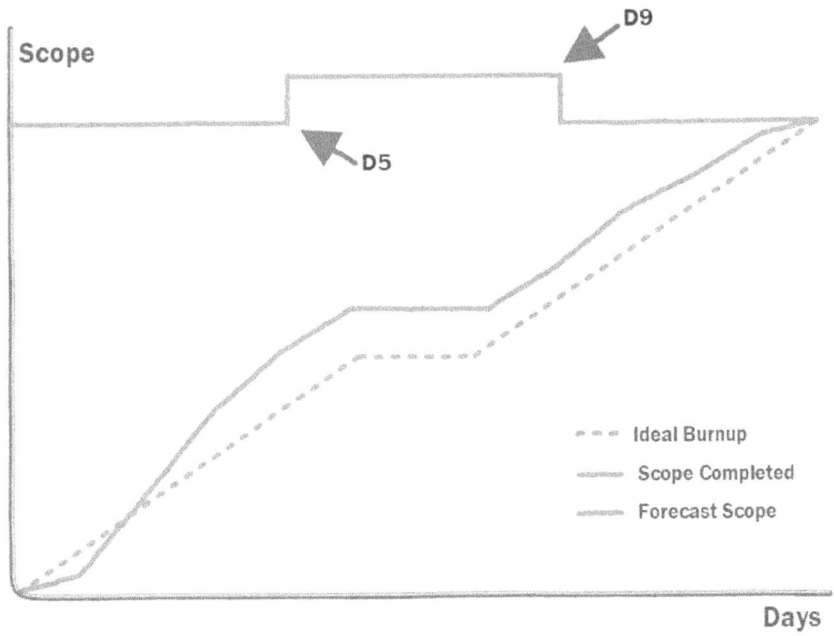

FIGURE 10: SPRINT BURNUP CHART

To sum it all, unless your team uses a tool auto-generating a Sprint burnup chart, you may want to leverage such chart to track and monitor the progress made on a product release or particular project only. Indeed, as the team conducts the Sprint, by simply attending the Daily Scrum, you should already know when user stories are being added or removed, and estimate the risks of doing so on the expected timeline of the product release or project.

3.11.7.4 Evaluate the Sprint Velocity

Velocity is a metric for the work done. It counts the number of units of work completed in a certain interval. In Scrum, the velocity is used in planning sprints and measuring the team's ability to get the job done within a single iteration. The theory behind this metric is actually simple: the average velocity can help the team better estimate how many units of work – story points, days, or hours – can be completed during a Sprint, assuming the team structure and Sprint duration are kept constant.

To calculate the actual velocity of a particular Sprint, you simply need to add up the estimates - story points, days, or hours - of all user stories completed in the Sprint, and you have it! Can't be simpler, right? Even a fourth grader can do it!

And, to establish the average velocity, the actual velocity should be captured over multiple sprints; typically, 4 to 6 sprints. Once established, the Scrum team can leverage this information to plan the next Sprint as illustrated next page. The product owner and the project managers can also use it to predict when the product release and projects will likely be completed and ready to ship.

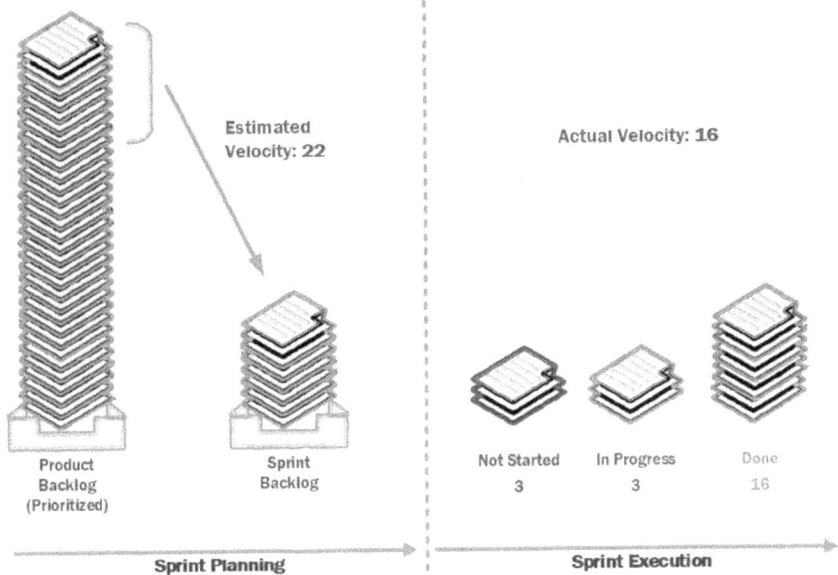

Estimated
Velocity: 22

Actual Velocity: 16

Product
Backlog
(Prioritized)

Sprint
Backlog

Not Started
3

In Progress
3

Done
16

Sprint Planning

Sprint Execution

FIGURE 11: SPRINT VELOCITY

If your product development team doesn't measure its velocity yet, you'd probably want to work with the Scrum master to start tracking it. The velocity might be a relative measure, but when used correctly, it can help you gain valuable insights into the progress and status of the product release and ongoing projects. It can help you as well in setting and communicating the right expectation to all the product stakeholders. Remember that everybody – product or project sponsors and executives – has a particular deadline in mind. So, be proactive, take the lead, and communicate the predicted target dates before anyone does it for you. You're the driver! You're in control. Trust me, velocity tracking is a precious forecasting tool you do want to add to your toolbox.

Last but not least, it's important to note that measuring velocity doesn't ensure better planning, better predictability, and improved throughput. There are indeed several flaws in using velocity because, as said in the previous paragraph, it's a relative measure. What does it mean? Consider the following situations:

- If you communicate the velocity metric as a performance indicator, the team may start over-estimating the effort required to complete a user story, thus, artificially increasing its velocity
- If you measure the Scrum team performance through its velocity, the team may cut important corners in the product design, forgo the agreed quality standards, ignore the Definition of Done, or postpone addressing the technical debt

Thus, as you begin tracking the velocity, be careful not to solely rely on it for planning sprints and forecasting product release and project completion dates. Instead, use it as another indicator along with the other tools we discussed earlier to plan the future sprints and evaluate progress.

3.11.8 Inspect and Adapt the Potentially Shippable Product Increments

Congratulations! The Sprint has now ended! It's time to inspect the product increments that have been built and delivered. It's time for the Sprint Review ceremony.

The Sprint Review brings all the product stakeholders in the same (virtual) room to review the completed product increments, share information and provide feedback on the developed features, and to consequently increase the product's market shares and penetration. Obviously, you, as the product owner, have a pivotal role to play here. You are, needless to say, the person accountable for the Sprint deliverables. You're the one who decides if the delivered product increments can be shipped or not...

Keep in mind that the Sprint Review is not only a meeting where the Scrum team demonstrates the Potentially Shippable Product Increments developed during the Sprint, it's also a meeting that provides all product stakeholders the opportunity to inspect, discuss and adapt the developed product increments.

The Sprint Review meeting typically starts with you, the product owner, going over the goal of the current Sprint and the Sprint Backlog. The

Scrum team then presents the state of Sprint Backlog Items, and, as appropriate, demonstrates the completed product increments that are ready to be possibly released.

During the meeting, all attendees are invited to ask questions regarding the developed features and provide feedback. The attendees also share information on internal and external environmental factors that may influence the features of the Product Roadmap, the user stories currently being developed or to be developed in the near future. The attendees may recommend enhancements to adapt to the new or evolving business needs. Throughout the ceremony, the participants identify risks and potential mitigation action plans, and escalate technical constraints if need be.

As per design, the Sprint Review doesn't have a formal structure. It is meant to be a horizontal and vertical bidirectional communication platform to transparently review the current state of the developed product including scope, timeline, and budget.

While the Scrum master facilitates the Sprint Review, your role is also essential. Throughout the meeting, you must be engaged, ask probing questions to the Scrum team and product stakeholders, validate the business assumptions made before or during the Sprint, and confirm the product increment meets all agreed acceptance criteria. If it does, great news! You have a product to ship. If it doesn't, you reject it, and start working with the Scrum master and the team to capture in the Product Backlog what's missing to satisfy the original request.

Once all product increments have been inspected and a clear decision has been made to either accept or reject the deliverables, you can wrap-up the meeting, and invite the Scrum master and the Scrum team to join you for the Retrospective.

3.11.9 Learn from the Past Sprint

You own the Product Backlog, you're the lead and facilitator of the Backlog Grooming. You're also the person driving the sprint goal and priorities for the next Sprint, and are accountable for the product delivery and for its return on investment. For all these reasons, you do have a major stake in the Sprint Retrospective and should do your best to attend. The objective of this meeting is indeed to improve the product development processes and the applied Scrum framework, and in consequence, accelerate time to benefits.

Having said that, since the product owner has de factor an authoritative position, your attendance might be counterproductive if you don't agree and commit to the ground rules for participating; rules that the Scrum master has laid out for all attendees. No exception! Why? Because in the end, you too want the team to succeed, don't you? And to do so, all the team members need to be able to share their opinion without being scared. Assist the Scrum master in creating a trusting environment, in which all participants can discuss sincerely (and bluntly) what went well, what could have been improved, what they would like to continue doing, start doing, or stop doing. Thus, before the meeting even starts, ask the Scrum master to communicate (over-communicate I should say) to everyone that they all belong to the same team. Help all attendees understand that you're neither the boss nor the patriarch. You're just a team member! The Scrum master may say it differently but, you get my point: Leave your ego at the door.

On that *friendly* note, there is a lot you can do to help the team conduct a successful retrospective. To name only a few:
- Let the Scrum master facilitate
- Embrace your participative role
- Be an active participant but don't monopolize the meeting
- Volunteer to be the first to share your thoughts about the Sprint if no one else does
- Answer as candidly as possible when you're asked a question
- Don't shy away from a tough problem (especially if you're responsible)

- Don't finger-point if a problem occurs during the Sprint
- Collaborate with the team to dive into the root cause of problem
- Ask open-ended questions to the participants
- Don't interrupt the person who is speaking
- Accept the constructive critics regarding the processes you own and manage
- Provide constructive inputs and feedback
- Collaborate with the team to identify actionable improvement measures
- Don't judge a new idea or suggestion
- Commit to the recommendations the team agrees upon

Last, once the Retrospective is completed, and the team goes on and starts working on the product backlog items of the next Sprint, don't let the ball fall. Be accountable and follow-up on any action items and/or process improvements assigned to you.

3.12 Monitor the Release

To make a long story short, monitoring a product release is the same as monitoring a project[7].

You, the product owner, are responsible and accountable for the return on investment. You must ensure the costs to manufacture the product will be positively offset by the benefits of delivering it; i.e.: you must make sure that the product will increase both revenue and profit of the organization. And, it's doesn't matter if you use an Agile methodology, such as Scrum, or a plan-driven methodology to develop your product. In the end, you're still accountable for the financial success of product.

---

[7] A project is "*a temporary endeavor undertaken to create a unique product, service or result. A project is temporary in that it has a defined beginning and end in time, and therefore defined scope and resources.*" Definition from the Project Management Body of Knowledge (PMBOK®) Sixth Edition, by the Project Management Institute (PMI®)

Keep in mind that Agile is not about doing what you want, when you want, regardless of the cost. In both Agile and plan-driven methodologies, you must appreciate and recognize the typical triple constraints: Cost, Schedule and Scope.

You (especially when no project manager is assigned to the release) should always keep the project within the agreed boundaries as documented in the Release Plan. And doing so amounts to monitoring and controlling the product release and its set constraints.

If you went-up the ladder within the same company to become the product owner – like I did before switching to technical project management — you may not have known that you had to at least understand or at best master the project management discipline... But, now you know!

The Project Management Body of Knowledge (PMBOK®) Sixth Edition describes the Project Management disciplines into five process groups and ten knowledge areas.

The **five** project management **process groups** are:
1. **Initiating:** Define a new project or a new phase of an existing project by obtaining authorization to start the project or phase
2. **Planning:** Establish the scope, refine the objectives, and define the tasks and actions required to achieve the objectives
3. **Executing**: Get the work defined in the project management plan completed to satisfy the requirements
4. **Monitoring and Controlling**: Track, review, regulate the progress and performance of the project, identify any areas in which changes to the plan are required, and initiate the corresponding changes
5. **Closing:** Complete or close formally the project, phase or contract

---

The **ten** project management **knowledge areas** are:

1. Project **Integration** Management: Identify, define, combine, unify, and coordinate the various processes and project management activities within the Project Management process groups
2. Project **Scope** Management: Ensure the project includes all the work required, and only the work required, to complete the project successfully
3. Project **Schedule** Management: Manage the timely completion of project
4. Project **Cost** Management: Plan, estimate, budget, finance, fund, manage, and control costs so the project can be completed within the approved budget
5. Project **Quality** Management: Incorporate the organization's quality policy regarding planning, managing, and controlling project and product quality requirements to meet the stakeholder expectations
6. Project **Resource** Management: Identify, acquire, and manage the resources needed for the successful completion of project
7. Project **Communications** Management: Ensure timely and appropriate planning, collection, creation, distribution, storage, retrieval, management, control, monitoring, and ultimate disposition of project information
8. Project **Risk** Management: Plan, identify, analyze and monitor risks, plan and implement the appropriate responses
9. Project **Procurement** Management: Purchase or acquire products, services, or results needed from outside the project team
10. Project **Stakeholder** Management: Identify the people, groups, or organizations that could impact or be impacted by the project, analyze the stakeholder expectations and their impact on the project, and develop the needed management strategies for effectively engaging stakeholders in project decisions and execution.

We'll further discuss the project management process groups and how they relate with the phases of an Agile project in a future volume (Scrum Management: A Day in the Life of... a Project Manager). But, for the time being, let's narrow down our focus on the monitoring and controlling process group – since it's what brings us here in the first place: figure out how to monitor the release...

According to the PMBOK® Sixth Edition, the *"Monitoring and Controlling Process Group consists of those processes required to track, review, and regulate the progress and performance of the project; identify any areas in which changes to the plan are required; and initiate the corresponding changes.* **Monitoring** *is collecting project performance data, producing performance measures, and reporting and disseminating performance information.* **Controlling** *is comparing actual performance with planned performance, analyzing variances, assessing trends to effect process improvements, evaluating possible alternatives, and recommending appropriate corrective action as needed."*

As part of this process group, the project manager monitors the progress made by the team on the project activities (i.e.: actuals vs. planned), evaluates change requests, monitors risks, and decides the appropriate response.

This process group involves processes belonging to each project management knowledge area as illustrated next page:

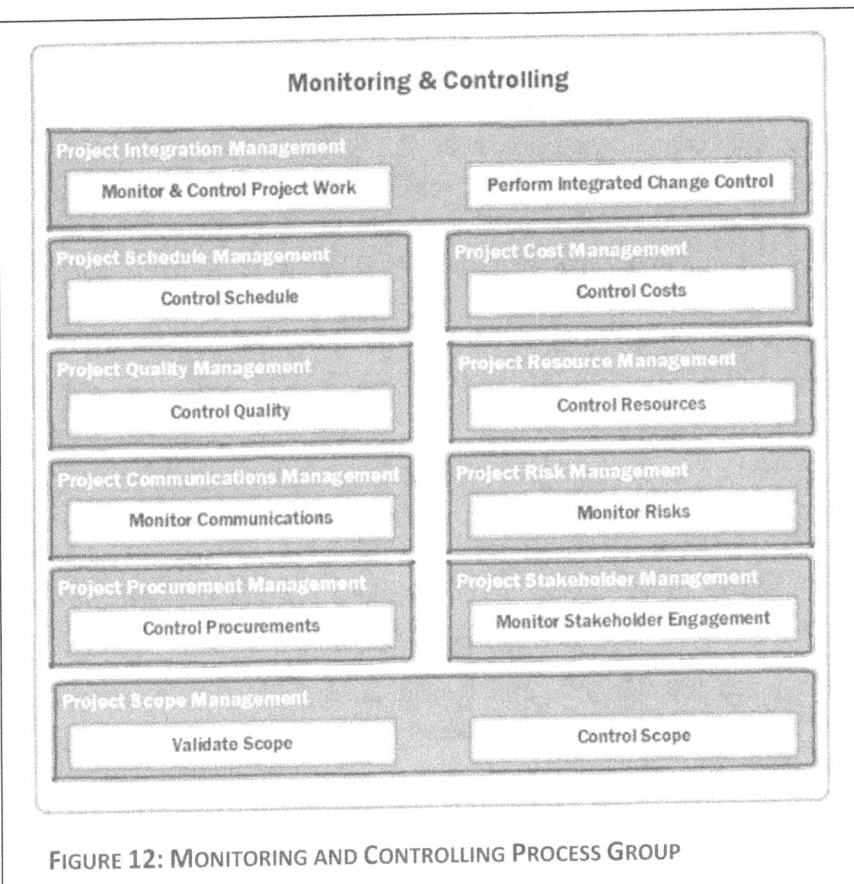

FIGURE 12: MONITORING AND CONTROLLING PROCESS GROUP

Without deep-diving into each process, which will require an entire book, the key objectives and outcomes of monitoring and controlling process group can be simply stated. These are to (a) assess if the work required to deliver the product release is on track, and (b) implement the necessary corrective actions to avoid or reduce delays, scope creep[8], and cost overruns. The project manager implements these processes through a set of tools and techniques.

---

[8] Scope creep refers to changes, continuous or uncontrolled growth in a project's scope. It's the number one reason for projects to be delayed or run over budget.

The project manager must first define a baseline as discussed in the project management plan and establishes the methods that will measure and capture the current project data so that the project manager can analyze and compare actuals with the baseline. Depending on the knowledge areas being monitored and controlled, the project manager can leverage various data analysis techniques, such as alternatives analysis, cost-benefit analysis, root cause analysis, variance analysis, reserve analysis, what-if scenario analysis, performance reviews, stakeholder engagement assessment matrix, trend analysis, earned-value analysis, Sprint burndown charts, etc.

The Earned Value Analysis is surely the preferred technique to monitor and control the project scope, schedule and costs. It enables the project manager to compare the planned value (i.e.: what the team should have completed at a particular point in time), the earned value (i.e.: what the team manages to get completed at this given time), and the actual cost (i.e.: what the team truly spent to attain the earned value).

As discussed earlier, Sprint burndown charts are valuable tools to visualize how the currently committed work is being completed. To monitor the progress on the current product release, you can use the same technique. It's best, however, in my humble opinion, to use a release burnup chart. The release burnup chart will indeed allow you to visualize more easily any scope creeps or potential delays.

For instance, in the Figure 13: Product Release Burnup Chart, next page, you can observe that:

1. Early in the project, the team made great progress. Up to Sprint #6, you may have even envisioned completing the release ahead of schedule.
2. However, during Sprint #7, the team faced challenges and its velocity dropped. During the retrospective, you asked the team if something was missed. You then worked with the Scrum master and the team to make the necessary changes right away.
3. The implemented changes benefited Sprint #8. The team proceeded with no impediment and continued being ahead of schedule.

4. Unfortunately, in the next two Sprints, the velocity dropped again. You began worrying as the project seemed to no longer be ahead of schedule. You were now right on schedule. During the retrospective, you talked to the team and tried to get to the bottom of it. The team explained they've been working on the most complex user stories of product release, and they planned on completing them next Sprint. You decided to attend the daily scrum to better support the team and monitor more closely the progress done.

5. During the next Sprint, the team demonstrated its ability to deliver on schedule.

6. In the next Sprint kick-off, the team indicated the release date would be delayed by a couple of weeks because of defects identified late in the Sprint #11. You informed the product stakeholders about the schedule changes, and proceed forward.

7. Sprint #13, following a successful Sprint Review, you decided that product release can finally be shipped!

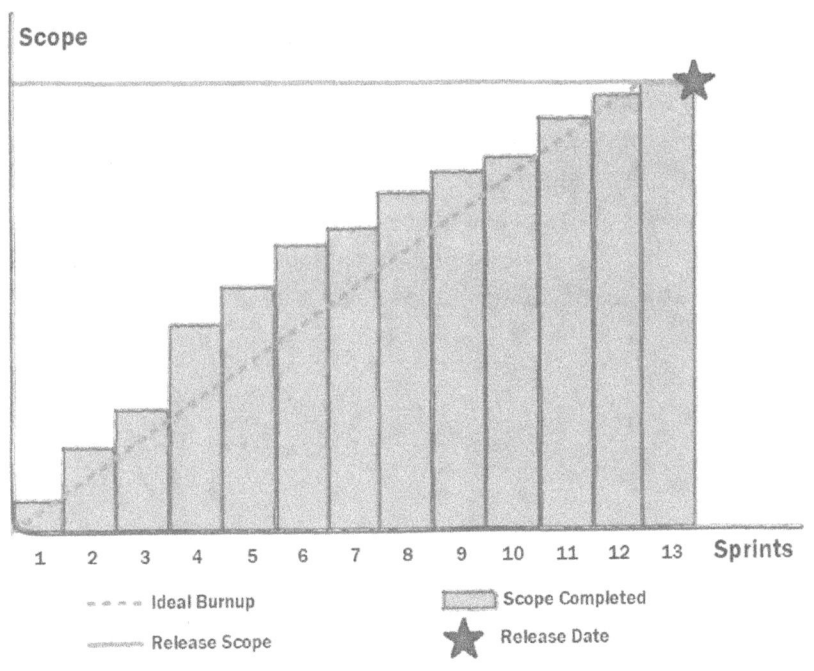

FIGURE 13: PRODUCT RELEASE BURNUP CHART

The release burnup chart is a useful tool for the team as it provides visibility and helps you track the progress toward a given release date. You can plot the completed scope as line, or as illustrated in the previous figure, as a histogram. It's your call!

The forecasted scope (shown as a horizontal line) helps you spot where and how much work is being added or removed (the horizontal line will go up or down). It's also a powerful and effective communication tool to use in your project status reports. It's your tool to adapt and use to best communicate bi-directionally: vertically to the project sponsors and executives, and horizontally to your peers and coworkers. Remember that the product release burnup chart illustrates clearly if the release scope is stable (under-controlled) or not, and if you're on track to make the anticipated release date.

Last but not least, monitoring and controlling the release also imply that the engagement of all product stakeholders at the appropriate level, and it's your job to make sure it happens. For example, if the product release is targeted for a particular customer, and the expert end-user assigned by the customer to answer the product development team's questions is not available, the product release is most likely going to experience challenges. It's once again your role and responsibility to measure the engagement level of each stakeholder, and assess if changes must to be made. This requires you to possess strong soft skills. You should know how to listen, negotiate, influence, lead, and network.

3.13 Drive the Product Quality Requirements

The magic word is out: Quality! Who doesn't aspire delivering the best product possible? Who doesn't want to build a product with the highest quality, a product the customers adopt, embrace and recommend to their friends and relatives? We all do. But, who is actually responsible for ensuring that the released product does satisfy the expected quality? Well, everyone is! Everyone involved in the design, development, validation and release of a product is indeed responsible. Quality management is the output of an entire team's work. But, as always, even though quality is everyone's responsibility, only one person is considered accountable. And guess what! It's your luck; it's you – the product owner!

Now that you know and appreciate that you're the accountable person for the overall product quality, the one product sponsors, executives, customers, and end-users will come to if there is a problem, what does it mean for you?

First, you need to have a high-level understanding of what quality management is and what the primary anticipated outcomes should be. Let's start with a definition: *"Quality Management: ensures that an organization, product or service is consistent. It has four main components: quality planning, quality assurance, quality control and quality improvement. Quality management is focused not only on product and service quality, but also on the means to achieve it. Quality management, therefore, uses quality assurance and control of processes as well as products to achieve more consistent quality."* The primary anticipated outcomes of quality management activities are then obvious: (a) meet the customer requirements and (b) strive to exceed customer expectations.

All of that is great, right? But, agreed, I have yet to discuss the actionable steps you should consider to drive the product quality requirements. So, here they are:

1. **Represent the Voice of the Customer**: you should have a good grasp on the customer needs and expectations. Go back to the section 3.11.5 (page 85) if need be

2. **Ensure the Project Quality Management processes are applied to the product release**:
    a. Plan Quality Management: identify and set the quality policies, standards and requirements applicable to the release. Document how these requirements will be measured, monitored and controlled in the Quality Management plan.
    b. Manage Quality: Capture the identified quality metrics, and execute the needed activities to keep these metrics within the agreed standards
    c. Control Quality: Assess the performance of implemented quality activities, and adjust these activities as appropriate

    For more information, explore the FAQ: What is Quality Management? (Page 156), and don't shy away from reading the PMBOK® Guide Sixth Edition.
3. **Manage the Technical Debt**; see next section
4. **Manage the Definition of Done** (page 112)

3.13.1 Manage the Technical Debt

The technical debt is *"a concept in software development that reflects the implied cost of additional rework caused by choosing an easy solution now instead of using a better approach that would take longer."* This concept can be extrapolated from the software development domain and describes simply as a financial debt. When you apply for and get a loan, you must repay the loan amount, along with interests. So, the sooner, the faster you repay the loan amount, the better since interest payments won't accumulate. Well, in product development, it's the exactly same!

When time is of the essence, we tend to take shortcuts. Instead of doing it right the first time, we opt for the easiest design and solution. We take the easiest path, which typically comes with errors, throwaway work, and a certain inability to adapt. It implies re-work and a need to refactor. It means the team will have to resolve defects and other unknowns that could surface and will inevitably have to be addressed further down the line.

Thus, every day you'll face and deal with the same dilemma: what should you prioritize? Should you develop a new feature or resolve a known defect? Should you request the team to complete a critical epic targeted for the present release or, postpone the release to reduce the technical debt?

Your job is to weigh-in the pros and cons of each user story (new feature, change request, defects, re-factorization activities, etc.) and prioritize the Product Backlog to maximize both short-term and long-term return on investment of the product. Just remember that even though everyone (and especially your company executives and project sponsors) wants to release the product as soon as possible, you should do your best to maintain the quality standards set in the Quality Management Plan.

Any compromises on quality may end-up costing you and the team way more than you think. And, do you really want to spend all your time and energy during the next few Sprints repaying the increasing product technical debt? My guess is: you don't.

So, make the right call! And, keep in mind that it's always better to do it right the first time, even if you have to explain to your sponsors and executives that the release is slightly delayed or over-budget. It might seem like a tough pill to swallow, but trust me, you'll spend way more to resolve a known defect after the product gets shipped...

3.13.2 Manage the Definition of Done

The Definition of "*Done*" (DoD) is used to drive the product development processes and product quality; this means the DoD lists the set of development activities that are required to deliver the solution. Nevertheless, the DoD is not set in stone. It evolves over time along with the Scrum team's ability to navigate the different phases of product development model, the feedback received from the end-users, and the complexity level of customer requirements. And, since you're the person accepting or rejecting the Sprint deliverables, you're in control!

This control should however be based on two ground rules: (a) the acceptance criteria of a backlog item and (b) the mutually-agreed overarching product development definition for when a backlog item can be considered completed (i.e.: the DoD).

Because the Acceptance Criteria are specific to the Backlog Item and typically leaves no place for interpretation, it's fairly straightforward to ascertain whether the delivered product increment meets the criteria or not. On the other hand, the DoD can at times be opened for review and interpretation. This is where you come in! This is where you can influence the team to move from an ambiguous definition to a more comprehensive list of activities that can be quantitatively and qualitatively measured.

For example, your Definition of Done could currently include the following:
- The developed changes have been peer-reviewed and signed-off by a Senior Product Engineer
- The developed changes have been captured in the Configuration Management System
- The Product Increment has been validated by and signed-off by the Product Testing team
- The product owner has approved the release

The listed activities might be sufficient in the early stages of a product. But as the product evolves, gains market shares, and crosses the chasm, you'd likely want to make changes to the above DoD to consider additional product development activities, such as:

- The Low-Level Product Design has been produced, reviewed and approved by a Principal Engineer
- The product increment has been demoed and successfully validated by Beta Testers
- The Product Documentation – Testing documents, Release Notes, User Guides, etc. – has been updated, reviewed, and approved by the product owner and product marketing manager(s)
- All product deliverables have been reviewed and approved by Legal and Public Relation

It's your job to drive the DoD toward a comprehensive list (or checklist) of activities that would improve the product quality and reduce the risks your organization could face should the product ships with major defects. But, don't worry. You're not the only one who has these ideals and concerns in mind: both the Scrum master and the team aim at the same objectives.

3.14 Avoid the Common Mistakes

You and I are the same. We are both human beings. And, like everybody else, we make mistakes. It's our nature. It doesn't really matter how hard we work or try to be perfect, and excel into our life, we always end-up doing something wrong. Admitting this truth is not being negative or pessimistic. It's being humble, and honest with ourselves. Everyone makes mistakes. The sooner we accept it, the better.

Luckily, we also have an incredible ability to learn from our missteps, study the failures of others, adapt to constant changes, and find our own path to move forward. As long as we appreciate that (a) nothing is certain, (b) perfection is never attainable, (c) delivering a product is a journey with its ups and downs, and (d) as long as we can avoid repeating the same common mistakes, we can always achieve the personal or professional goals we set for ourselves.

That said, a list of common traps product owners often fall into is enumerated below:

- **Think and Manage in Silos:** if you don't understand and embrace *transparency*, a foundational principle of Agile, and spend your time and energy building horizontal or vertical silos between people, you fail in your role and core responsibilities. In fact, if transparency is not one of your inner strengths, you should very seriously consider doing something else! Do your best in sharing information and ensuring the Product Backlog and all non-confidential Product Release documents are accessible to the product development teams.

- **Be Unavailable and Disengaged:** The Scrum team trusts you as the sole Voice of the Customer. They rely on your availability and engagement throughout the Sprint to assist in removing impediments and clarifying the customer requirements and expectations. Be engaged, be present.

- **Have Others Direct or Assign Work to the Scrum team:** In organizations new to Scrum, the product owner generally fears challenging the functional dotted-lines between managers and the team. And, as a result, this leaves doors open for others to assign work to the Scrum team. This also leads the Scrum team not to attain the sprint goal since the team doesn't solely work on the Sprint backlog. Talk to whoever asks the team to do something and direct them to submit their request through the Product Backlog. Empower the Scrum team to say "No" when a request wasn't made through the Product Backlog. Educate all parties about the purpose of using the Product Backlog; it helps prioritizing the work and making sure the team doesn't burnt-out due to unplanned requests.

- **Be Indecisive:** Not only do you represent the customers, you're also the person accountable for the product release. The team counts on you to decide promptly so the work can proceed forward with minimal or no delays. Be careful though! *Promptly* doesn't mean you must decide now and without data. It just means that you shouldn't delay a decision if you already have the required insights.

- **Under-Communicate:** To align all parties engaged in the product development activities, you must spend sufficient time to communicate, coach and share your vision for the product with everyone. Why do you think Project Managers spend 90% of their time communicating? The more you communicate, the more people understand and adhere to the Product vision, the clearer the business priorities are, the easier your work will be: Communicate, communicate, and communicate again. I cannot emphasize it enough.

- **Initiate a Sprint without Planning:** Before the team kicks-off a Sprint, you should prioritize the Product Backlog, refine the *Must Have* User Stories, and ascertain the sprint goal to achieve. Not doing your due-diligence would waste everybody's time, lead to uncertain Sprint results, and ultimately lower your return on investment.

- **Engage in side-conversations during a Scrum ceremony:** There is nothing worse and detrimental to a meeting than having attendees engaged in side-conversations. Not only do they not contribute, but they also disturb the other participants. Lead by example. Assist the Scrum master, if need be, in keeping everyone focused on the issue to discuss and resolve.

- **Arrive late to the Daily Scrum:** The Daily Scrum is 15 minutes long. So, what's the point of attending if you can't make it on time? You might be the product owner but, you can't do f#$k without your team. Respect everybody's time. Show-up on time.

- **Try to solve an impediment during the Daily Scrum:** The Daily Scrum is not a problem-solving session. You may have good intentions in diving into and tackling a particular issue or impediment during the meeting, but don't! Instead, let the team know that you're available right after the meeting to discuss the user story, and resolve any associated concerns or roadblocks.

- **Ignore the Sprint Retrospective:** There is a purpose to all Scrum ceremonies. There is no point to meet if no objective is attained. The Sprint Retrospective is used to learn from the past and subsequently improve how the product is being developed. It's your best interest to follow-up and see through any action items, continuous improvement initiatives, or recommendations surfacing from the retrospective.

3.15 Have a Balanced Life

By now, you should have all the tools you need to become a successful product owner:

- You understand the role and responsibilities of a product owner
- You have great insights into the customer needs and expectations
- You have a clear and articulated product vision and roadmap
- You know how to communicate this vision to all product stakeholders
- You can obtain the buy-in from all the stakeholders
- You're empowered and trusted by your organization to make the right decisions
- You take full ownership of Product Backlog
- You efficiently and effectively collaborate with the Scrum master
- You're active and engaged during the Sprint
- You assist the Scrum team to clarify requirements and remove any impediments
- You inspect, adapt or accept each built product increment
- You continuously look for areas of improvement in the product development processes
- You avoid all the too common mistakes
- You approve the release

There is no doubt you'll love your job and enjoy delivering the best experience possible to your customers through the product and service you and your team will be building. As you learn on how to drive the product in the best direction, it'll be very easy for you to get consumed by the sole passion of what you do. It's actually normal. If you love what you do, you won't even notice the time passing by. But you should as well do your best to live a balanced life.

Early in my own career, I was so committed to the product I managed that I failed to realize that the hours I was spending at work were not sustainable. I was working more than 100 hours per week. Every day, I arrived in the office early and left late in the evening. And, one day a week, I was not even leaving the office! From June 2008 to May 2010, in addition to my typical extended working hours, from Wednesday morning to Thursday late afternoon, I was pulling a 40-hour work shift. As expected, these demanding working hours helped me to grow as person and manager. I learned a lot about my physical and mental abilities. But, I learned the hard way. And, I could have avoided a few missteps, starting with better managing my own backlog, and fully embracing the agile manifesto and one of its key principles:

Sustainable development, able to maintain a Constant Pace

What does it mean?

It means that you need to be smarter than I was in my early career. Remember to favor consistence over anything else, and never forget that a job isn't everything in life. Life is much more! We all have family and friends. They too deserve our love and time. And, drawing from these words of wisdom, I'll leave you here since I'm confident that you'll find the balance you need, and make your own path to:

- Apply successfully all you've learned to design, build and deliver the product your customers need,
- Love collaborating with product development teams and customers,
- Do it without sacrificing quality time with your loved ones.

Please, have a balanced life.

4 Frequently Asked Questions (FAQ)

This FAQ dives deeper into some of the terms and concepts discussed in the previous chapters.

4.1 What is the Business Model Canvas?

The Business Model Canvas or BMC is a template designed to give you a quick, simple and single-page structure to develop, refine and implement your business plan. It captures the essence of your company or product by focusing on nine distinct and essential building blocks. It helps you align your organization and team activities by illustrating potential trade-offs. These nine building blocks will assist you in articulating the who, the why, the what, and the how.

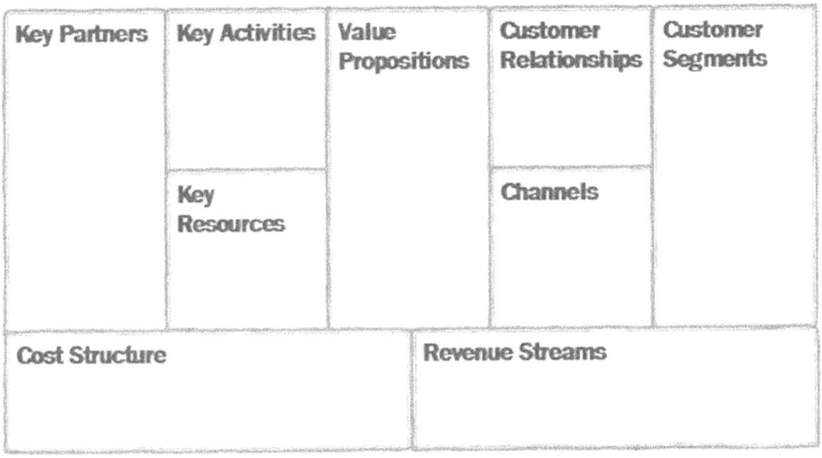

Key Partners	Key Activities	Value Propositions	Customer Relationships	Customer Segments
	Key Resources		Channels	
Cost Structure		Revenue Streams		

FIGURE 14: BUSINESS MODEL CANVAS

Before diving into how to use this structure to quickly and easily shape and refine the vision of your company and product, let's first talk about the basics: the nine foundational elements of this canvas.

4.1.1 Customer Segments

Because customers are and will always be at the center of your business, the BMC always starts with the customers. To build an effective business, you should never lose track of deviate from why you do what you do. Your goal should be to provide value to your customers. And to deliver value, you need to understand who your customers are, what they do, what they see, what they feel, what they think and, most importantly, what they want and need to achieve their own professional or personal goals and dreams.

When brainstorming on these questions, consider the various sets of customers you want to serve. Are you targeting the mass market or a niche market? Do you want to build a multi-sided platform that will service mutually dependent customers? Do you want to diversify your offerings so that you can address the needs of a wide range of customer types? Or, do you prefer focusing on a specific (and perhaps very familiar) segment of the population? There is no right or wrong answers here. It's all about who you want to assist through your products and services.

Once you have nailed down the customer segments you want to serve, dive deeper, and try personifying each segment by defining user personas. The more you know about your customers, the more you can personalize and visualize who they are, the better position you are to develop the right product or service. The better position you are to articulate the value you can provide to these customers.

4.1.2 Customer Relationships

Because you've done your homework and understand who your customers are, you should now be able to determine the type of relationships you want to establish with them, and determine how to best interact with them. These points of contact should guide your customers throughout the end-to-end journey of using your product or service.

Do your customers (and defined user personas) prefer indirect interactions with self-service capabilities? Do they rather have a personalized and dedicated assistance during and/or after the sales process? How do they want to obtain information on new or product updates? Would they trust feedback or insights from other potential and existing customers?

As you think about these questions, place yourself in the customer's shoes and, consider the different and possible situations your customers may want to interact with you and your company: request for information, informal or formal pre-sales activities, product or service pricing negotiation, during the actual sales, while the product is being shipped, when the product or service is being installed at the customer's location, request for assistance (question, troubleshooting, etc.) after the sales, etc.

These various potential interactions are opportunities for you to not only acquire customers but also to build a lasting and mutually beneficial relationship. And don't forget the old adage: it takes time to gain the customer trust but, it only takes one mistake to lose it forever. It's therefore critical to never lose side of the big picture and long-term vision you have for your company and products.

4.1.3   Value Proposition

Now that you know who your customers are and how to best communicate and interact with them, it's time to dive into the why: why would a customer buy or use your product and not another one? What's so appealing about your message and product? What's the added value of your offering? What's the value proposition of your product or service? And, how different is it from competitors?

In 1998, Michael Lanning and Edward Michaels defined "value proposition" as *"a clear, simple statement of the benefits, both tangible and intangible, that the company will provide, along with the approximate price it will charge each customer segment for those benefits."* But, to make a long story short, your value proposition should communicate to your customers the benefits they'll gain by purchasing, subscribing and using your product or service. You message should give them a sense of direction, create focus and confidence, and help them distinguish your company and product from competitors and competing offers. Nonetheless, don't fall into the sales speech trap! Your value proposition should not only attract potential customers, it should remain truthful and provide honest and tangible answers to your customer needs.

Once you can articulate the advantages and benefits of your product or service, and once you understand the drivers that would convince customers to adopt your solution, you're half-way there! Remember that even though the value proposition is a simple statement, crafting a short and concise statement is not an easy task, especially when this very short statement needs to communicate how your product is (a) different, (b) better and (c) worth purchasing. And if it helps, keep in mind that your value proposition may capitalize on quantitative or qualitative factors, such as price and efficiency gain. Take a look at the below impactful value proposition examples:

- MacBook: *Light. Years ahead.*
- Spotify: *Soundtrack your life.*
- Vimeo: *Make life worth watching*

To come up with such creative and meaningful value proposition statement, I usually advise the product owner to conduct design thinking workshops with focus groups representing the targeted customer segments. These workshops will assist you, the product owner, in drafting robust statements that will deliver a compelling experience and ultimately drive and motivate the new customers to buy the product, and, consequently, increase sales and revenue.

4.1.4   Channels

At this time, you should understand who your customers are and have a good grasp on the value proposition of your products or services. Now, you need to figure out the best method to communicate, promote, sell and deliver your propositions to your customers. You need to determine the Channels that should be used to maximize your reach and benefit the most your bottom line.

As you brainstorm with your team or ideate on your own, you should think about the various touchpoints you're going to have with the customers and/or customer segments: How do you plan to inform your potential customers and raise awareness about your products and services? How are you going to assist the customers in selecting the right product (the product you offer)? How will you guide them through the purchase experience? How will you deliver the purchased product or service? And, how will you support the customers after the sale?

Below is a non-exhaustive list of channels you can consider for specific goals:

- Raising awareness of your product, service or brand:
  - Word of Mouth
  - Traditional Media: Newspaper, Radio, Television
  - Social Media: Facebook, YouTube, Twitter, Instagram

- Assisting in the selection and evaluation of your value propositions:
  - Reviews
  - Questionnaires
  - Surveys

- Purchasing your product or service:
  - Online Retail
  - Brick & Mortar

- Delivering the purchased product or service to the buyers:
  - Direct delivery
  - Picked-up at a Brick & Mortar
  - Downloadable product

- Providing after-sales support to the customers:
  - User Community support
  - Online Customer Service
  - Call Center

As you evaluate your options, keep in mind that the best channels are fast, efficient and cost effective.

4.1.5   Key Activities

There are many common-sense, apparent and logical activities a business must perform to ideate, position, design, build, market, sale, deliver and support its products or services. But, what are the unique and must-do activities your business does to supply its peculiar value proposition? These key activities are the ones that make your company stands out, that constitute its core competencies.

As you identify and develop your key activities, try analyzing, decomposing and reviewing your company's activities through the industry-agnostic Business Process Framework eTOM[9]. And do your best to focus on its specificities.

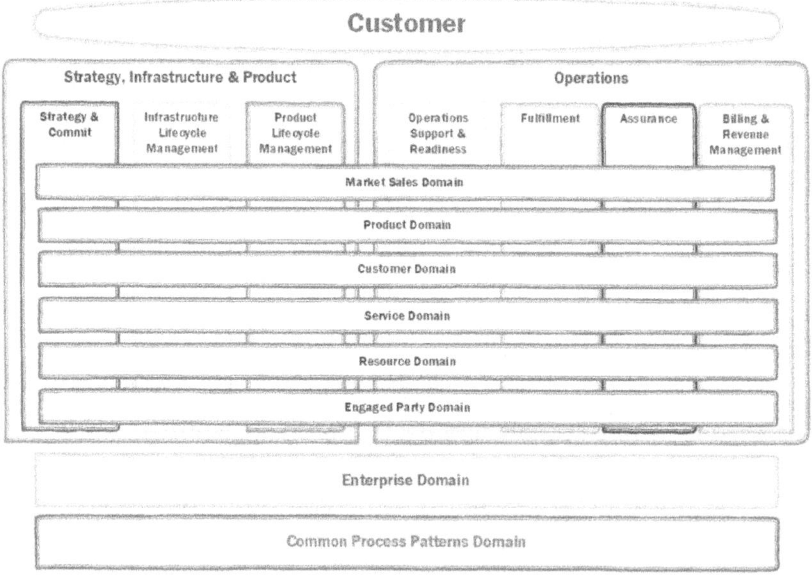

FIGURE 15: ETOM BUSINESS PROCESS FRAMEWORK (16.5 MODEL)

---

[9] The enhanced Telecom Operations Map (eTOM) is a Business Process Framework that describes and analyzes different levels of enterprise processes according to their significance and priority for the business. The framework is defined as generally as possible so that it remains organization-, technology- and service-independent. eTOM is a standard maintained by the TM Forum: https://www.tmforum.org/

4.1.6   Key Resources

A company cannot create and deliver added value to its customers without employing and applying resources to implement its key activities. When identifying the Key Resources your business needs, carefully consider the previous blocks we discussed earlier:

- The Customer Segments you want to establish and foster lasting relationships with
- The Value Proposition your business creates and delivers
- The different Channels needed to reach, connect and engage with your customers
- The Key Activities required to create and deliver your products or services.

Remember as well that these Key Resources can be physical (buildings, vehicles, computers, etc.), intellectual (patents, brands, knowledge domain expertise, etc.), financial (cash, stock, credit line, etc.) and human. They can also be owned by the business or simply acquired from the Key Partners.

4.1.7   Key Partnerships

Often, an organization needs to partner with other businesses to achieve its vision. Collaborating with others can lead to many benefits. Partnerships optimize operations, reduce risks, exploit opportunities, and help you focus on your core competencies. Key Partnerships may include relations with governmental entities, strategic alliances with competitors, joint ventures with non-competitors, and contractual agreements with buyers, suppliers and/or distributors.

As you develop your business model and refine the value propositions you want to bring to customers, consider creating partnerships in areas that drive your focus away from your key Activities.

4.1.8   Cost Structure

It is time to discuss and dive into the costs of doing business! And, because you now have a good handle on your business model and its value propositions, you should be able to ascertain if your company is cost-driven or value-driven:

- A **cost-driven business** aggressively manages and minimizes all costs – through outsourcing, supplier and partner management, automation, etc. – so that it can create and deliver its products and services at a highly competitive and lowest price possible.
- A **value-driven business** is less concerned with costs as it concentrates on (a) establishing its brand in a niche market or non-competitive environment, (b) creating and delivering the highest value possible to its customers, and (c) exceeding its customer needs and expectations.

So, do you want to run a cost- or value-driven business? Once you can articulate, decide, and defend the answer, the next step is to determine the costs of your Key Resources, Activities, Partnerships and Channels (i.e.: the major costs drivers) of your business.

As you make an inventory of your costs, remember the two major cost types:

- **Fixed Costs** are costs that do not change. Examples are salary, rent, loan payment, etc.
- **Variable costs** are costs that do change; e.g., manufacture costs, delivery fees, etc.

Once all costs have been inventoried, make hypotheses on these costs, and estimate them. The more you know about the costs that your company will incur, the best position you will be in to (a) create and deliver the products and services you want to bring to the market, and (b) determine the viability of your business model.

According to several studies, 50% of start-ups fails within 5 years, and 75% within 10 years. Why is the failure rate so high? One of the top seven reasons is dramatically simple: it's the failure from entrepreneurs to correctly determine and estimate the cost structures of their business. Sad, right?

Shikhar Ghosh, Professor of Management Practice in the Entrepreneurial Management Unit at the prestigious Harvard Business School, studied and analyzed more than 2,000 Venture-backed Start-Ups and found that up to 75% of them failed to realize the forecasted return on investment, and return cash to their investors.

In short, as you dive into your company cost structure, be careful. Be diligent... No pressure! *(sync)*

4.1.9   Revenue Streams

Customer Segments, Customer Relationships, Value Proposition, Channels, Key Activities, Key Resources, Key Partnerships and Cost Structure are no longer unknowns to you. You have them figured out and documented in your business model canvas. The final step is to determine if you have a viable, profitable, and sustainable one! Piece of cake, right? After all, before even forming a business, you should already have an idea on how you'll earn revenue, how you'll make a profit. I concur, it's not that simple. So, let's take it one step at a time.

Revenue is, as everyone knows, a Key Performance Index of a business. Luckily, there is a legion of means to generate revenue and ensure the sustainability and profitability of your business.

Revenue can fall into two categories:

- **Non-Operating Revenue**, which refers to the money earned from (a) interests on financial placements or on investments such as debt owned, (b) dividends from holding stocks of other companies, or (c) rent revenue (when it's not the company's main industry).
- **Operating Revenue**, which originates from the company's core business operations. The rest of this section focuses solely on Operating Revenue.

Recurring Revenue is the preferred revenue stream of companies because it's predictable income! It provides a consistent inflow, which primarily depends on the size of company's customer base. Recurring revenue streams include:

- Hard contract; e.g.: a cell phone carrier's two-year contract, a ten-year lease agreement
- Auto-renewing subscription; e.g.: a monthly membership, software as a service,
- Licensing fee; e.g.: yearly fee to use a protected intellectual property
- Sunk-money subscription; e.g.: a one-time membership installment fee
- Straight-up subscription; e.g.: a one-year subscription to a print magazine or newspaper
- Sunk-money consumable; e.g.: a desktop ink printer
- Simple consumable; e.g.: an ink cartridge

Transaction-based Revenue is derived from seasonal products or services. It's therefore challenging to predict this revenue type. For example, camping gears sales boost during the summer, but typically go flat during winter. Most brokerage, usage or advertising fees fall under this category as they depend on transaction volume.

Service Revenue is generated from providing time-based services to a customer. This revenue type is typically billed by hours, such as consulting services.

Project Revenue is the most risky and volatile revenue stream as it is contingent on a unique endeavor to build and deliver to existing or new customers. Businesses will invest a fair amount of time to manage customer relationships, ensure the customer needs and expectations are clear, understood and can be met by the solution being developed. Businesses often put in place strict monitoring and controlling processes to guarantee the financial success of executed projects.

So, how does your company make money?

Through the definition of different Cost Structures, you should now have determined if your company is a cost- or value-driven. This should greatly influence how to look at your revenue streams.

On one hand, if you run a cost-driven business, your revenue stream will heavily depend on your sales volume. That means that your products or services are purposely priced low to retain existing customers or acquire new ones from competing offers. Thus, the larger quantity you'll sell, the more revenue you'll generate.

On the other hand, if you run a value-driven business, the same is obviously true. But, in addition, you must understand the value you actually create for your customers. You can then associate the added value with the physical price your customers will be willing to pay for the product or services.

Similar to the exercise you did for the cost structures, you need to make hypotheses on your revenue streams and estimate each stream. You will then be able to determine – comparing estimated costs and revenues – if you should go back the drawing board or proceed forward with your business model.

4.2   What is Design Thinking?

The easiest way to describe and explain Design Thinking would be to cut corners and tell you that Design Thinking is about *"thinking outside of the box."* But this won't help you move the needle in the right direction, right? So, let's take a different route, a route that provides you a fairly comprehensive description of what it is:

> Design Thinking is an iterative process in which the customer is at the heart of everything. Hence, if your company is customer-obsessed, Design Thinking is a tool you'd most likely be interested in discovering and applying to define, design, build, and deliver an innovative and quality product.

Having said that, before describing any further what exactly this process is, let's clear the table of all misunderstanding and misconception: Design Thinking is not bound to a particular industry. It's simply an iterative and powerful problem-solving approach to product design and development. And, like everything in life, while people may agree on the approach, there is rarely a consensus on how to implement it.

In this section, I am going to focus on the 5-phase process taught at the Hasso Plattner Institute of Design at Stanford, commonly known as the d.school. These phases are: Emphasize, Define, Ideate, Prototype, and Test. Figure 16: Design Thinking Process illustrates this process.

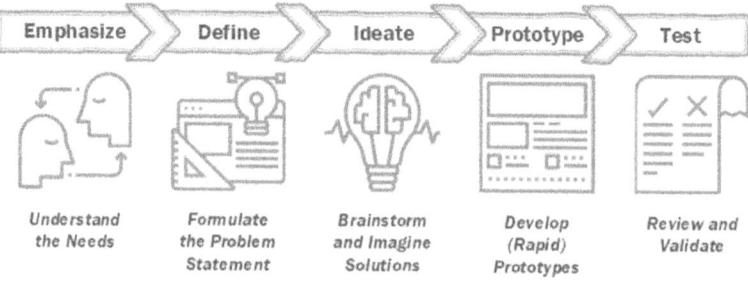

FIGURE 16: DESIGN THINKING PROCESS

And, as you look at this diagram, don't get stuck in the constructed dimension, as highlighted below:

1) The phases of this process don't follow any particular order: they can be executed sequentially, in parallel, or even skipped

2) Results from one iteration feed the next one

4.2.1   Emphasize

As mentioned earlier, the customer is at the heart of Design Thinking. Without knowing who your customers are, without understanding their needs and desires, without developing a certain level of empathy with your target customer segment(s), you'd likely (and I should in fact write "*surely*") miss the point. You'd design a product that won't find its audience and never cross the chasm. So, in this phase, your goal is to understand the end-users for whom you develop this unique product. And, the best way to achieve this goal is to spend time with your customers and interview existing or prospective customers.

The more you know, the better you understand, the better decisions you can make. Customer interviews are critical to gain valuable insights into the drivers, motivations, and behavior of customers. They can also highlight questions and issues you never thought about. That said, interviewing customers is an art of its own as there are many traps to avoid falling into. And the first traps are actually the easiest to elude by doing the following: (a) be prepared, (b) know your domain, (c) forget any presumptions you may have, (d) ask open-ended questions so that interviewees can speak freely, without constraints and barriers, and (e) plan to have a fun and open conversation! Keep in mind that your goal is not to reach a particular conclusion or solution. Interviews are meant to collect customer insights, and understand pain points, challenges, needs and wants.

There are several types of interview: face-to-face, over the phone, online questionnaire, survey, etc. Each approach has its own pros and cons. For example, face-to-face interviews are most effective to dive deep but they are also time-consuming and more expensive than conducting an online survey. So, as you plan and initiate this phase, pick your poison, and do your best to understand where your customers come from, what problems they face, how they really use the product, what they need and why, what the barriers to make a purchase are, etc.

And while you consider the types of interview you'd prefer conducting and who you should interview, let me stop here and leave you with sample questions that may assist you in this critical phase:

- How did you find the product? How did you learn about the product?
- What made you purchase the product?
- What does our product help you do? How do use the product?
- What do you feel when using the product? Can you help me understand your feelings better? Are you happy about your purchase? Do you regret your purchase?
- Have you ever faced a problem with the product? How often did you face this problem?
- How much have you spent to resolve this problem?
- Where do you find information about the product? Where do you search first and find answers for a problem about the product?
- Did you ever have to contact customer support for the product? What do you think about the support you received? What makes you feel that way?
- Would you recommend the product to a friend?
- Which improvements would you recommend to the product? Which improvements would help you the most in using or purchasing your product?

4.2.2   Define

Following the *Emphasize* phase, you should now have a good understanding of the needs and wants of your customers. You should have a firm grasp on the problems they face, and on the needs they express. In this phase, you're going to dive deeper in the needs to fulfill and the problems to resolve. You're also going to articulate a set of objectives to achieve, such as a features list or a price point. You're going to define the problem through the definition of a problem statement. This statement should help the product team framing the work to be done…

What's a problem statement? You may ask. Well, it's *"a concise description of an issue to be addressed or a condition to be improved upon."* A problem statement includes a vision (the ideal state), describes the current state (the reality), explains the issue or gap between the current state and desired state (the consequences), and discusses possible methods to solve the problem (the proposal).

As you work on developing your problem statement, do your best answering the usual W's: Who, What, Where, When and Why. Don't be afraid to ask may questions and dive into the why! Question the problem. Question any hypotheses. Questions any assumptions. And, question yourself if this is indeed the correct issue to resolve, the desired gap to close? The deeper you can dive into the issue, the better your chances of identifying the real problem. Remember that no one knows it all. Understand that the true issues are difficult to pinpoint. And this is the reason why you need to conduct this phase as a group exercise.

The unique working session(s) should conclude when all participants agree on the ideal state, the current reality, the central issues to resolve, and the high-level proposal, which will be used to address the problem. But, this isn't the end of this phase! Before turning the page and move on, you must craft a clear, concise, and accurate statement to steer and direct your solution in the right direction. This statement will also help you deliver the expected product and results.

Oh, yeah! Before you even ask about the How, don't worry! You'd answer the how in the next phases.

4.2.3   Ideate

In the *Define* phase, you initiated the process of coming-up with possible methods to solve the problem. In this phase, you're going to put everything back on the table, and generate as many ideas and options as possible to resolve the problem. Yes! It's time to be creative and brainstorm! And while brainstorming, remember that there is no right or wrong idea. Design Thinking is about *"thinking outside the box"*, right? So, think and sketch various solutions by looking at the problem from various perspectives. Ideate, ideate and ideate! And, don't be concerned about the number of ideas you might generate. You'll have plenty of time later to triage, prioritize and vet each idea. Plus, good ideas would naturally rise to the top.

4.2.4   Prototype

In the *Ideate* phase, you had fun coming up with various ideas. But, if creativity brings joy, then turning concepts into reality will bring even more joy. And here, in this phase, this is exactly what you're going to do! It's time to develop and build a prototype. But, where to start? Which idea should you consider first? My answer might be too simplistic, but, still, try using the MoSCoW prioritization technique again. For information, this technique is discussed in page 139: What is the MoSCoW Prioritization? And if you're still uncertain, weigh-in the business impacts, the anticipated added value for the customers, and the fit within the overall problem statement. Consider as well the level of complexity and effort that will be required to prototype the selected idea(s).

Once you decide which ones are worth prototyping, the next step cannot be *simpler*! You *just* need to coordinate the activities of Product Development teams to design and develop the *infamous* prototype(s)! First, you must communicate clearly the objective of prototype. In this phase, you are not building the final product. Your goal is more modest. You want to turn an idea into something that can be tested fast, discarded or pushed through the product development processes. You want to build something that you can potentially build on, iterate, and refine to deliver a Minimum Viable Product. The resulting MVP should then address the original problem statement.

4.2.5   Test

In the *Prototype* phase, you turned an idea into a tangible solution. But does this solution bring answers to the real problem? Does this solution meet the end-user expectations? What can you learn from the developed prototype? What works? What doesn't? It's time to find out if you're on the right track, or not.

This Testing phase is all about validating the developed prototype(s) and getting unfiltered and raw feedback from the end-users to better understand the delivered experience. As such, it can be a difficult phase for the inventor you aspire to be. Critics can be tough to handle, especially if they aren't constructive. But that's what you want: unfiltered feedback from you direct end-users. So, as you absorb and analyze the received inputs, it's only human that you might feel overwhelmed. You might even want to throw the towel and give up. Don't! Instead, remember what Thomas A. Edison wrote in 1877: *"Many of life's failures are people who did not realize how close they were to success when they gave up."*

Design Thinking can be challenging as your *best* ideas might be harshly shut down by customers. Hence, it's key to continuously keep an eye on the end goal. Mistakes will be made. Accept it. Embrace it. Failing is a natural step of creation. Learn from these customer feedback. Learn from your failures, and incorporate them into the next prototype you'll be developing. Understand as well that there is no perfect solution. And, at one point in time, you'll have to decide if the problem has been *sufficiently* resolved, and pull the trigger so that your prototype could be further refined and transformed into the future MVP you'll be excited to bring to the market.

4.3   What is a SMART Requirement?

A functional or non-functional requirement should always be accurate, clear, unambiguous, unique and verifiable. To better determine if a requirement is a "good" one, the product development industries borrowed the SMART acronym from project, performance or personal development management. A SMART requirement is Specific, Measurable, Achievable, Relevant, and Time-Bound.

- **Specific**: The requirement is unique and describes with unambiguity, simplicity and with the appropriate level of detail a new feature or enhancement to develop. The description of the requirement should be easily understandable and should avoid any possible misinterpretation.
  - X Bad: The Product should provide different permissions access to end-users
  - ✔ Good: The Product should support an end-user with read-only access only

- **Measurable**: The requirement describes quantitatively (preferably) the anticipated outcome so that the delivered solution can be factually verified and validated by the Testing team, and accepted by the product owner and customer.
  - X Bad: The Product should support several concurrent read-only users
  - ✔ Good: The Product should support up to 50 concurrent read-only users

- **Achievable**: The requirement describes a feature that is reasonable and attainable (given the existing circumstances). Attainable means it is physically feasible for the product to actualize the requirement.
  - X Bad: The Product should be always available
  - ✔ Good: The Product should have a 99% uptime guarantee

- **Relevant**: The requirement should be aligned with the Product Vision and, directly connected to its primary intent. As the sole owner of the Product Backlog, the product owner is best placed to assess if a particular requirement is relevant or not.

- ✗ Bad: The Product will generate over 1 million sales
- ✓ Good: The Product will be ranked in the top-10 on search engines

- **Time-Bound**: The requirement specifies a particular timeframe by when or how fast the requested action should be completed or executed.
  - ✗ Bad: The Product should display quickly the main page after the end-user successfully logs in
  - ✓ Good: The Product should display in less than 4 seconds the main page after successfully logging in

4.4 What is an Acceptance Criteria for a Backlog Item?

Traditional and Agile Product Development share a key need: the capability to validate and accept the delivered product, solution or service against mutually agreed criteria. Defining the Acceptance Criteria for a Product, Product Increment, User Story, Backlog Item or Work item is critical and an integral part of the Product Development methodology.

When the Product Backlog Item is defined as a SMART requirement, Acceptance Criteria provides additional details to the Scrum team to ensure the Backlog Item and Product Increments can be considered as complete, and ready for formal testing. Acceptance Criteria should be determined prior to the Scrum team picking up the Backlog Item. It is the responsibility of the product owner to ensure that only Backlog Items with clear Acceptance Criteria are added to the Sprint Backlog, because in order for the Scrum team to consider the Backlog Item complete, the Acceptance Criteria will provide them with accurate and precise business, functional and non-functional requirements, and leave them no room for interpretation.

Once a solution has been developed to address a requirement, the Tester or Quality Assurance Engineer validates the solution against the documented Acceptance Criteria of the associated Backlog Item, developing the necessary test cases (and automated unit tests) to confirm the produced solution meets the documented needs. Hence, Acceptance Criteria should describe quantitatively as much as qualitatively the expected outcome.

4.5   What is the MoSCoW Prioritization?

Moscow is surely the capital of Russia but, it's also a mnemonic to help remembering four categories of priority: Must, Should, Could, and Won't (at this time). This prioritization technique is used in project and product development to acknowledge the importance of all requirements, differentiate the wants from the needs and dreams, as well as ensure the product development teams focus first on the requirements delivering the greatest business value.

Each team and company must determine and then agree on its own definition of each priority. Below are possible (but commonly adopted) definitions:

- **Must Have** requirements are critical for the current timed-box delivery, the project success and the product increment acceptance. These requirements define a Minimum Viable Product (MVP); a product with the necessary features meeting the critical wants of end-users and customer.

- **Should Have** requirements are important for the project success but not necessary in the current time-box delivery and product increment acceptance. These requirements are often as essential as *Must Have* Requirements but are not time-critical; the end-users and customer can wait for a future delivery as they have an acceptable workaround to achieve the desired outcome.

- **Could Have** requirements are desired features that would improve the overall end-user experience with the product. The product owner often decides to prioritize these requirements in a future delivery if: the development cost is low, the product development teams have the bandwidth, and the customer satisfaction would increase significantly.

- **Won't Have *(at this time)*** requirements are the requests that all stakeholders have agreed not to deliver. These requirements may have a high development cost for a very little added business value, or are not appropriate or consistent with the current state of the product.

Throughout the Product Lifecycle, the product owner re-assesses the priority of each Backlog Item.

4.6 What is a Good Backlog Item?

In 2003, Bill Wake developed a checklist evaluating the quality of a user story. This checklist can be condensed in the acronym: INVEST, and can be applied not only to user stories but to all backlog items.

INVEST stands for:

- **Independent:** The Backlog Item should be self-contained, and could be implemented independently from others.

- **Negotiable**: Since collaboration is a core value of Agile methodologies, a Backlog Item should be open to discussion, and the final technical decision on how to implement the requested requirement made by the Scrum team.

- **Valuable**: The product owner prioritizes a Backlog Item by weighing among other things, the business value of the underlying Product Increment that will be delivered to the end-users, customers and stakeholders. During each Sprint, the Scrum team should work on the Backlog Items delivering the highest value.

- **Estimable**: The product owner, solution lead and Scrum team should understand thoroughly a Backlog Item, to evaluate its complexity and size it. A Backlog Item is first estimated in Story Points and then in hours once the Scrum team has decomposed it into Sprint tasks.

- **Small**: The size of a Backlog Item should allow the Scrum team to deliver a solution to the requirement with an iteration. If a Backlog Item is too large to be completed during a Sprint, the Scrum team should decompose it into smaller items.

- **Testable**: A Backlog item should have well-defined Acceptance Criteria so that the Scrum team can best assess if an item is ready to be tested. This means that the anticipated outcome should be quantitatively and qualitatively measurable for the developed Potentially Shippable Product Increment to be validated.

4.7 How to Write a User Story?

Fresh from a restful night, you wake up this morning with an idea in mind for the product you have a stake in. This idea might be a brand-new functionality or a feature you notice doesn't work as expected. After a healthy breakfast, and a short commute to work, you settle at your desk and start writing down your idea. You submit it into the Product Backlog and you move on with your day with a certain sense of accomplishment.

A week later, out of the blue, you're informed that the requirement you submitted has been rejected. The product owner is asking you to re-write it so that the product development team can act on it. You're baffled, and frankly, a little frustrated. You ask yourself why they didn't get it. Wasn't the requirement clear enough? You go back to the idea you submitted, and review the comment added by the product owner before rejecting it: *"please re-write the requirement as user story."* **User Story**! Here it is, the magic (and evil) word!

You ponder for a few seconds and, have a lightbulb moment! You've just remembered that Mark, one of your colleagues, have a strange book on its shelf; the **Scrum Management**: *The Agile Practitioners Survival Guide*.

You open it and read the following explanation:

> ... A **User Story** is a statement which embraces a specific structure or template in order to present a need. Note that having a consistent template to document a User Story helps the Scrum team to understand better and faster the requirement.
>
> The most popular template, developed in 2001 by a team at Conextra, is: "As a <role>, I want <goal/desire> so that <benefit>." The "so that" clause is optional. With the introduction and adoption of the Persona concept, many Agile practitioners have opted to describe a User Story using the following format: "As <persona>, I want <what?> so that <why?>."

You now understand why the product owner rejected your idea. The Scrum team expects all Product Backlog items to have the same well-defined structure to more easily understand the requirement. This resonates with you. It makes sense! Your earlier frustration goes away, and you dive into your original idea so that you can submit it as a User Story. But, how and where to start? Well, you're in luck! This section is going to guide you, step-by-step, through the writing process of a user story:

- Step 1: Identify the Persona
- Step 2: Describe the Goal
- Step 3: Document the Benefits
- Step 4: Detail the Expected Outcome
- Step 5: Put It all Together
- Step 6: Submit the User Story

4.7.1 Identify the Persona

If you don't know who the requirement will be providing value to, you may want to stop right here. Think again. There's indeed no reason to spend time ideating, writing and submitting a user story without appreciating the person who, in the end, will leverage the delivered product increment.

A persona is a fictional character representing a user type. A persona leverages the product to achieve a very specific goal. The persona is typically developed with a real user in mind.

Assuming your product is a brand-new debit card for cryptocurrencies, called the `Freedom-Crypto Debit Card (FCDC)`, you may have determined three different customer segments and developed a persona for each segment:

- `The retired couple`
- `The young professional`
- `The road warrior`

So, do you have someone in mind? Maybe, the `road warrior`? Great! You have the "`as <persona>`" of your user story. The next step is to figure out the goal, the desire, the what, the "`I want.`"

4.7.2 Describe the Goal

What happens when a persona has no goal, no issue, or void? Is that a problem for you?

The answer is plain and simple: Yeah! If your customer has no goal, this implies two potential things:

- Your product is too perfect, too good. And, it'll very soon be obsolete, phased out, and be retired. In short, when your customer has no goal, you should do your best to innovate and create something novel that will drive again the demand. Needless to say, you can rely on the product marketing team to assist in this area.

- You don't know and understand enough your customers! Go back to the drawing board and refine your product persona. We all have aspirations and needs. They might not be materialistic. They might not be fulfilled by a new product feature. But, they might be satisfied through a different kind of service. Think about and elaborate on the desires of your customers. Envision what the best customer experience could be to meet these desires.

On the positive note, any product stakeholder can write and submit user stories. This means that you'll rarely run out of ideas for continuously innovating and enhancing your products and services. That being said, when it comes to writing the desire of the identified persona, stay away from the How! Instead, document the expected customer experience, the journey, and what the persona is looking for. In my experience, it always helped to complement this journey with some type of visual representation, a mock of the expected delivered experience. You don't necessarily need to include it in the first draft of user story but, it'll definitely help understanding the What.

For example, considering the road warrior, the desire can be:
a. I want to withdraw cash from an ATM (selling available bitcoins)
b. I want to deposit cash into my account at any ATM

4.7.3   Document the Benefits

You now have the "as <persona>" and the "I want." Next is the "so that", the reason why the specific desire exists in the first place. Writing the reasons, the benefits, the value for the persona should be the easiest part in writing the user story. After all, you truthfully have a good handle on the Who and the What. So, the Why should come naturally to you.

Going back to our previous examples:

a. I **want to** withdraw cash from an ATM (selling available bitcoins) **so that** I can purchase items at any stores.

b. I **want to** deposit cash into my account at any ATM **so that** I can purchase additional bitcoins.

4.7.4   Detail the Expected Outcome

Having the user story written down is great, but that's not enough! For the user story to be acted on, you need to document clearly what the expected outcome should be, to document the acceptance criteria. Refer to the What is an Acceptance Criteria for a Backlog Item? (Page 138) for more information.

Diving into the first example discussed above, the acceptance criteria could be as follows:

1. The road warrior has a cryptocurrency or digital exchange account.
2. The account total value is greater than the amount to be withdrawn.
3. The road warrior has swiped and entered a valid PIN.
4. The requested amount and withdraw fees were debited from the account.
5. The ATM has dispensed the requested cash amount to the road warrior.
6. The road warrior has received an email with the detailed transactions.

4.7.5   Put It all Together

The User Story should ideally be short – for example, 3-sentence long – and precise. It should also be written from the perspective of the product persona. The User Story should focus on one single feature or functionality. If it's not the case, slice your requirement into smaller user story (see page 147 the FAQ: How to Slice a User Story?).

You can also leverage Ron Jeffries's 3C[10]:
- **Card:** If you're limited in space to write the user story – writing it down on a post-it for example - you'll no doubt have to keep it short
- **Conversation:** When you document the needs through the eyes of your product persona, focusing on what the customer experience to deliver should be, the best way to communicate the anticipated customer journey is typically through a conversation – or a set of sequential interactions – between the customer and the product or service
- **Confirmation:** Don't forget to capture the acceptance criteria of the user story

4.7.6   Submit the User Story

If you don't already know how to submit your user story into the Product Backlog, simply reach out to the product owner!

---

[10] The 3C was first introduced by Ron Jeffries in his book **Extreme Programming Installed**: https://amzn.to/2N4gkAj

4.8   How to Slice a User Story?

After writing and submitting a user story into the Product Backlog, the product owner first reviews and triages it (See Triage the Submitted Backlog Item (page 57). If the submitted user story makes the cut and is officially added to the Product Backlog, the product owner brings it forward into the next Backlog Grooming ceremony. At that time, the product owner, solution lead, Scrum master or Scrum team may request the submitter to slice the submitted and approved product backlog item into smaller user stories that can be delivered within an iteration.

If you've never sliced a user story into smaller items, don't you worry! There is always a methodology, a process that can assist you.

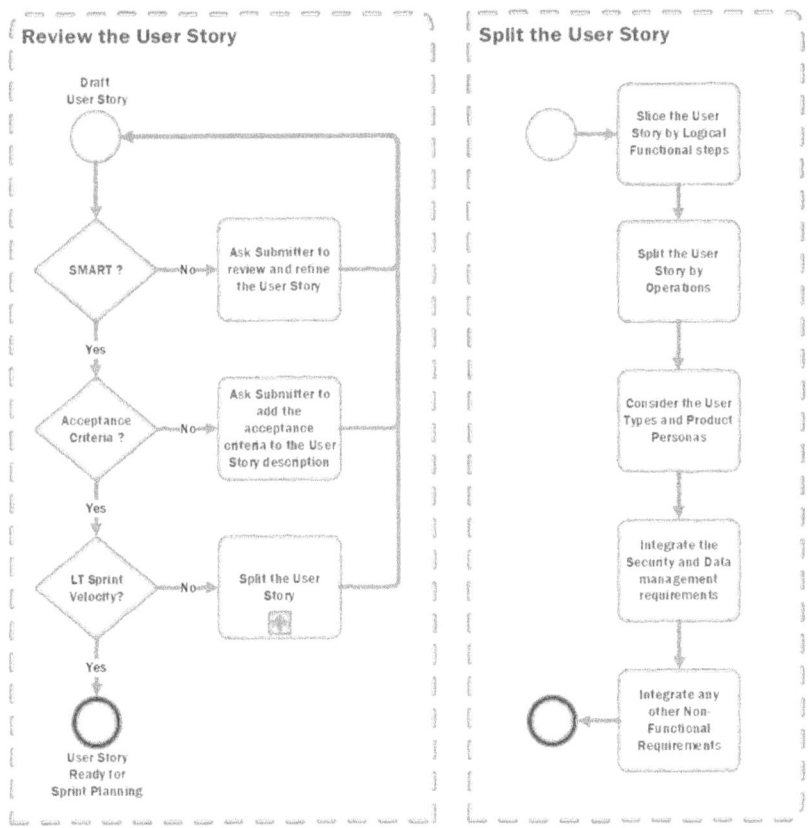

FIGURE 17: REVIEW AND SLICE A USER STORY

4.8.1   Review the User Story

In this step, the submitter of user story, which is being reviewed, doesn't necessarily have to do a thing! Cool, right? This step is indeed led by the product owner and is typically done during the backlog grooming ceremony.

First, the product owner and solution lead(s) validate whether the submitted and approved user story meets the SMART prerequisites - Specific, Measurable, Achievable, Relevant, and Time-Bound – or not. Refer to the FAQ: What is a SMART Requirement?(Page 136).

Second, the product owner and solution lead(s) validate the captured acceptance criteria will allow the Scrum team to easily determine if and when the future developed product increment that should address the requirement could be considered done and ready for delivery.

If the user story isn't SMART or doesn't have clear acceptance criteria, then the submitter still has work on its hands before the team can act on the idea: the submitter needs to go back to the drawing board, and refine the requirement and acceptance criteria.

Third, after the Scrum team has had the opportunity to size the submitted and approved user story, the product owner and Scrum master assess whether the estimated amount of work to complete the requirement is more than what the Scrum team can achieve within a Sprint; more precisely, the product owner and Scrum master check if the estimate of user story is greater than the team velocity, and in this case, well, it's time for you to split the user story!

4.8.2 Split the User Story

Here you are! You've just baked the largest chocolate chip cookie you've ever made, and you're ready to devour it with a glass of cold milk. But, this is when, for some reason, your parents, significant other or friends ask you to cut it into tiny pieces so that you can eat it safely without damaging your stomach. I can feel your frustration (being a cookie monster myself). Unfortunately, they are right. You have no choice and need to do it. You'd eventually understand that your stomach has a limited capacity and it will be unwise to go overboard.

Well, you see, in the Scrum methodology, it's the same thing. The Scrum team has a limited production capacity that is determined by the average Sprint velocity. For this reason, even though you may have submitted a valuable idea into the product backlog, you might need to slice it or break it down into smaller stories so that the team can act on it and build a complete product increment at the end of each iteration.

To split a user story, follow the process illustrated by the Figure 17: Review and Slice a User Story (page 147), and split the user story by

(a) Logical functional steps,
(b) Functional operations,
(c) User types or product personas,
(d) Security and data management requirements, and
(e) Other non-functional requirements (e.g.: performance, scalability)

If you still need further guidance, consider the actionable mind-maps shown next page.

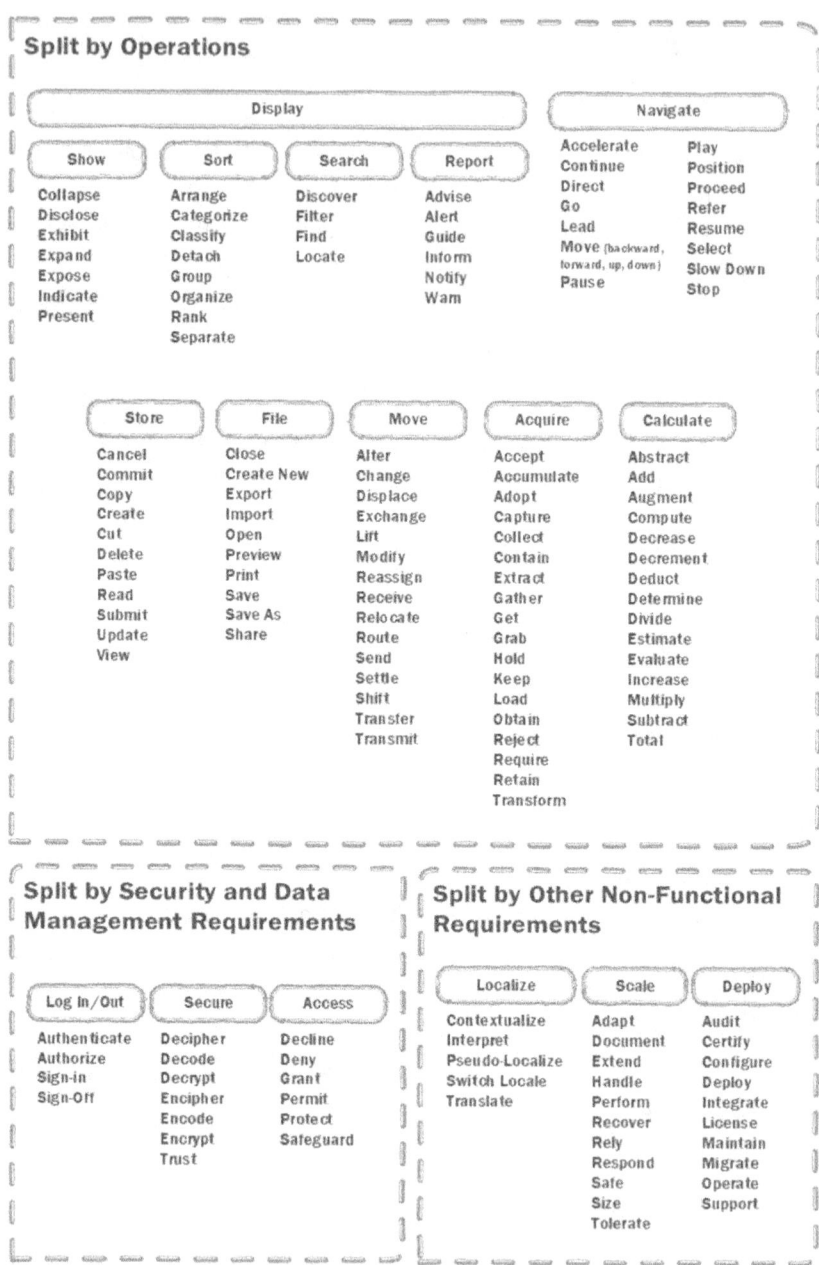

FIGURE 18: ACTIONABLE MIND-MAPS TO SPLIT A USER STORY

4.9 How are Product and Sprint Backlogs different?

The table below highlights the key differences between the Product Backlog and a Sprint Backlog.

	Product Backlog	Sprint Backlog
Ownership	Product Owner	Scrum Team
Creation	At Product or Project Ideation	At Sprint Planning
Content	All Product Features	Only items committed for completion within the Sprint
Estimate Unit	Story Points	Hours
Estimate Type	Is NOT a Forecast	Is a Forecast
Listed Items	User Story, Backlog Item, Business and Non-Functional Requirements, Change Request, Defect	User Story, Backlog Item, Business and Non-Functional Requirements, Change Request, Defect, Work Item, Training/ Learning Activity, Scrum Task
Editorial Permissions	Anyone, at Anytime, can submit an Item for the Product Owner to review, approve or reject.	Only the Scrum Team can edit the Sprint Backlog.
Review	Bi-Weekly or Weekly	Daily
Lifespan	Product (or Project)	Sprint

Table 5: Product Backlog vs. Sprint Backlog

4.10 What is a Minimum Viable Product?

"A Minimum Viable Product (MVP) is a product with just enough features to satisfy early customers, and to provide feedback for future product development" (Wikipedia).

In Scrum, the Minimum Viable Product is a technique used to decide when a Product and its Product Increments can be shipped. For a product to qualify as an MVP and be shipped, the product owner must validate that the product provides sufficient value for customers to purchase it, and has enough core features that would benefit adopters today and in the future. In addition, an MVP should ideally offer a mechanism to integrate customer feedback into future development and product releases.

4.11 What is the Release Planning ceremony?

This ceremony is not an official Scrum meeting. In fact, the name "*Release Planning*" is recently being debated among Agile practitioners, since many companies already ship every Sprint the generated Product Increments to their customers. There is however a consensus on the need for such meeting to help bridge the gap between the Product Vision, the Product Roadmap and the Sprint Backlog.

A Release Planning ceremony is a collaborative working session during which the attendees discuss the Product Vision, existing Product Roadmap, and Environmental factors to determine and agree on the scope and timeline of the next Product Release.

According to the Project Management Body of Knowledge (PMBOK®) Sixth Edition, Agile Release Planning "*provides a high-level summary timeline of the release schedule (typically 3 to 6 months) based on the product roadmap and the Product Vision for the product's evolution. Agile release planning also determines the number of iterations or Sprints in the release, and allows the product owner and team to decide how much needs to be developed and how long it will take to have a releasable product based on business goals, dependencies, and impediments.*"

This ceremony has one simple goal: to get from all attendees a commitment on the scope of the next product increment, and the timeline to take it to the market...

This goal is implemented through the actualizing of the following objectives:
1) Identify and understand the internal business needs and external environmental factors, placing greater emphasis on specific product features and functionality
2) Review the *Must Have* and *Should Have* Product Backlog Items, clarify and agree on the user stories, backlog items and requirements that will be included in the next release statement of work
3) Discuss any potential skill gaps that may need to be filled

4) Ensure that all parties involved have a clear understanding of the features and functionality that needs to be developed and delivered in the next Sprints.
5) Help craft the goal for upcoming Sprints

A typical agenda for a Release Planning session includes the following:

- Welcome and introductory roundtable
- Review the Product Vision
- Present the latest Product Roadmap
- Present the current Product Development status, including User Stories being worked on, assumed Technical Debt, previous Sprint results, past and forecasted Scrum team's velocity, etc.
- Present the current Business Priorities and current Market Competitive conditions that may place greater emphasis on specific requirements to be addressed by the next release
- Discuss and agree on the next release business, functional and non-functional objectives
- Review and clarify the *Must* and *Should Have* Product Backlog Items
- Understand the Technical Dependencies of Backlog Items that will most likely be part of the next Release scope of work
- Raise and discuss any potential skill gaps that would prevent the Scrum team(s) from building and delivering the discussed requirements
- Review the estimates of requirements, and agree on adding (or not) in the Release Backlog. (You may use the *"old-fashioned"* but always efficient post-its on the wall method)
- Determine the testing strategy, challenges and acceptance criteria for the Release
- Define a tentative schedule; and determine the required number of Sprints based on the Backlog Items estimates and Scrum team's productivity rate

- Discuss the goal of next Sprints and draft a strawman[11] to bring successfully to the market the planned release
- Get agreement from all attendees on the release goal, high-level scope and timeline
- Celebrate and adjourn the meeting

Note that during the session as the facilitator, the Scrum master (a) ensures all participants voice their point of view and concerns, (b) parks any topics that may require follow-up meetings, (c) captures any actions items, and (d) assists the product owner in achieving the meeting's objectives.

---

[11] A strawman is not an official artifact in Agile. In Scrum, a strawman helps the Scrum team to logically order the user stories and backlog items to be worked on over the next few Sprints. It's a rough proposal or map to move from ideation to delivery. Typically, the product owner revisits the strawman and release plan at the end of each iteration to incorporate the achieved Sprint results, and integrate new information into the release scope and schedule.

4.12 What is Quality Management?

How can you make sure the product, project or service you work so hard to build, offer and deliver will meet the customer needs and expectations? How can you reduce the risks of releasing a defective product? The answer lies within one core project management discipline called Quality Management.

Quality Management ensures that the inputs, processes, outputs and expected benefits are consistent with the requirements, fit the anticipated purpose of product or service being built, and meet a set of mutually agreed acceptance criteria (or quality requirements). Failure to satisfy these quality requirements implies that the developed product increments should not be shipped. And, if you decide to go ahead and still ship the defective product, it's likely going to result in serious negative consequences for your business and any or all of the product stakeholders. So, listen to the voice of reason and always abide by your quality requirements.

That said, before diving further into the four main components and the seven principles of quality management, let's define two very important terms that are often misemployed: *quality* and *grade*:

- **Quality** is *"the degree to which a set of inherent characteristics fulfill requirements"* (ISO 9000). It's a result, a conformance to the requirement, a delivered outcome
- **Grade** is *"a category assigned to deliverables having the same functional use but different technical characteristics"* (PMBOK® Guide Sixth Edition). It's a design intent

A Potentially Shippable Product Increment (or PSPI) that has low-quality should never be shipped. However, one of low-grade might not be a showstopper to ship. For example, a mobile application that has very limited functionality (low-grade) but has no defect (high-quality) might be the perfect tool for early adapters. Interesting concepts, right?

The good news is that the product owner is the one accountable for the overall product quality and, is the one deciding if the product can be released or not. This doesn't mean that the product owner will always strive to build high-grade and high-quality products and consider only the sky is the limit. Of course not! The product owner should know better. First, because perfection doesn't exist (there is no sky to reach). And, second, shooting for the stars ain't free! Quality has a cost...

"The cost of quality (COQ) includes all costs incurred over the life of the product by investment in preventing nonconformance to requirements, appraising the product or service for conformance to requirements, and failing to meet requirements (rework)" (PMBOK® Guide Sixth Edition).

COQ can be decomposed into two categories:

- **Cost of Nonconformance**: Costs spent during and after the product release because of failures
  - *Internal Failure Costs*: These costs are related to defects found by product team during the product development. Resolving these failures requires rework of the affected user story, and sometimes, it demands scrapping entirely the defective feature from the release.
  - *External Failure Costs*: These relate to defects found by the customers after the product release. These are the costs you should do your best and absolutely want to prevent! They include the time and effort required for the team to resolve the defects and ship a corrected product to the customers. In most cases, companies try offsetting these costs by offering their customers extended warranty or some type of premium customer support services. These costs also include indirect costs, such as liabilities, loss of customers trust, and lost opportunities and businesses.

  Failure costs are also called the costs of poor quality.

- **Cost of Conformance**: Costs spent during the product development activities to avoid failures and defects
  - *Prevention Costs*: These costs are driven by activities aimed at preparing and implementing a quality plan, and preventing poor quality. They include training, documentation, time to do it right. These costs might have been considered as fees to pay upfront one could opt to avoid. But, truth is, they are part of doing business and are typically more manageable than future

costs you may arise to resolve defects after the product release. They are also preferred and more predictable than the appraisal costs.

- o *Appraisal Costs*: These costs are incurred when you're testing, inspecting and auditing the developed product increments to (a) find potential defects, (b) demonstrate the established acceptance criteria are satisfied, and (c) ensure your Definition of Done has been met. The earlier defects are found in the development process, the less costly they are to fix. And, even better, preventing a mistake is always better and cheaper than inspecting and discovering defects before or after the product release.

  Cost of conformance are also called **Quality Control** costs.

The PMBOK® Guide Sixth Edition presents Quality Management in three distinct processes:

1. **Planning Quality Management** involves (a) identifying the policies, standards, and quality requirements applicable to the product, (b) documenting in the Quality Management Plan the metrics to consider, and how to capture, monitor and control them throughout the product development activities. The end-result of the Quality Management Plan process is to layout the framework that will achieve the quality objectives of product. In scrum, it's achieving conformity to the overarching Definition of Done as well as the Acceptance Criteria of each user story included into the product release.

2. **Controlling Quality** (aka Quality Control) is about measuring, sampling, auditing and recording the outputs and results of quality activities. Controlling also involves making adjustments to the quality specifications so that the product can be shipped as fast as possible while meeting the customers' needs.

3. **Managing Quality** (also called Quality Assurance) analyzes and leverages the metrics captured by the Quality Control activities so that the product being built can meet the customers' expectations. In Scrum, the artifacts, such as the Sprint burndown charts, are useful tools for this process. Managing Quality is also about

executing the required activities that identify ineffective processes, dive into the causes of poor quality, and recommend changes to achieve greater results.

The International Standard for Organizations (ISO) has adopted seven principles for Quality Management.

FIGURE 19: THE SEVEN PRINCIPLES OF QUALITY MANAGEMENT

These principles are the foundation of ISO 9000 and ISO 9001 quality standards, and are described as follows:
1. The primary focus of quality management is to meet customer requirements and to strive to exceed customer expectations
2. Leaders at all levels establish unity of purpose and direction and create conditions in which people are engaged in achieving the organization's quality objectives
3. Competent, empowered and engaged people at all levels throughout the organization are essential to enhance its capability to create and deliver value
4. Consistent and predictable results are achieved more effectively and efficiently when activities are understood and managed as interrelated processes that function as a coherent system
5. Successful organizations have an ongoing focus on improvement

6. Decisions based on the analysis and evaluation of data and information are more likely to produce desired results
7. For sustained success, an organization manages its relationships with interested parties, such as suppliers.

Source: https://amzn.to/2BX1QOx

Last but not least, quality is not an event or an activity to think about once in the product lifecycle. It's a constant. The product owner, the Scrum master, the Scrum team and all the other product stakeholders should strive to continuously improve how the product is designed, built and released. As mentioned earlier, perfection doesn't exist. There is always room for improvement. Thus, to the three previously discussed Project Quality Management processes, we need to add one more: **Continuous Improvement**.

There are several continual improvement methodologies. These include Six Sigma, Lean, Total Quality Management, Project Management Maturity Model, and Capability Maturity Model. But, as long as you appreciate that **Quality develops daily, not in a day**, there is no need for me to rehash what has already been said and written by many talented authors.

4.13 What is the Cone of Uncertainty?

In project management, the cone of uncertainty is a concept describing how unknowns and risks diminish throughout the project lifecycle. The idea is very simple. At the beginning of a project, you typically have very limited understanding of (a) the resources you'll need to reach the end-goal, (b) the tasks and the sequence you'll need to follow in order to complete them, and (c) the challenges and numerous surprises you'll face and force to manage. In fact, when you ideate and initiate a project, you basically know only one thing: the project goal; and not to scare you away from the project management discipline, very often, even the project goal evolves during the project life span. Fun, right?

As you progress and move from initiation to planning, from planning to execution, and from execution to closing, your knowledge on what to do and how to do it increases. Unknowns become knowns. Risks are deflected, realized, transferred or avoided. Opportunities are exploited, shared or they disappear in the thin blue air. As you learn more about the tasks to reach the project end-goal, you remove the sources of uncertainties. The estimates also evolve from rough order of magnitude to definite as discussed in the next FAQ (How do Estimates Evolve with the Product Development?). Hence, your decisions on the next steps to take for resolving the outstanding issues become more informed and confident.

And when you finally close out the project, there is no more uncertainty. You completed all required tasks, adjusted the scope and timeline, coordinating and getting the necessary buy-in from the project sponsors and everyone concerned. You revised the project budget so that all costs were covered and accounted for. You closed out all previously identified risks.

The Cone of Uncertainty depicts this natural evolution.

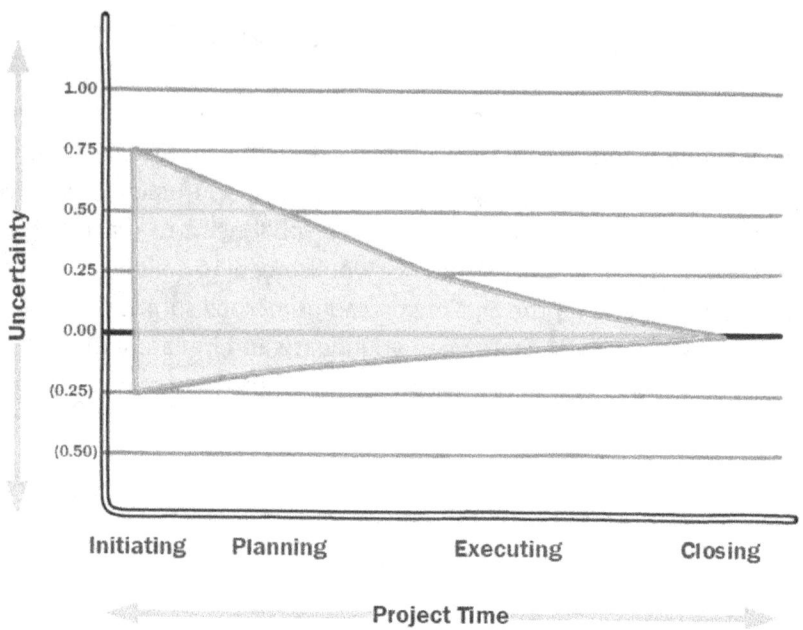

FIGURE 20: THE CONE OF UNCERTAINTY

4.14 How do Estimates Evolve with the Product Development?

Throughout the product lifespan, the development team continuously sizes and estimates the level of effort of each product requirement. The figure below illustrates how estimates evolve through time.

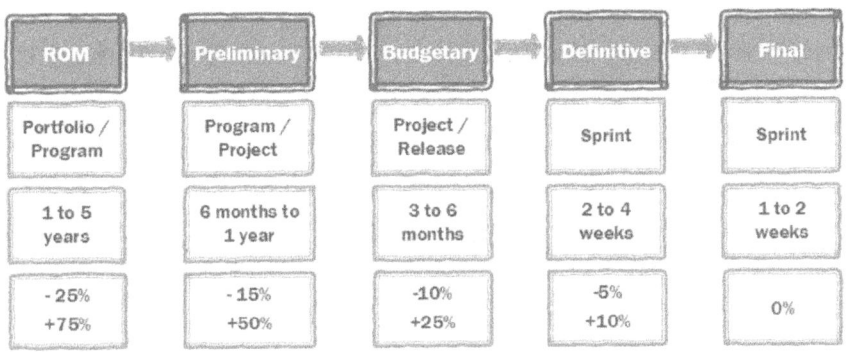

FIGURE 21: EVOLUTION OF ESTIMATES THROUGH TIME

4.14.1 What is a Rough Order of Magnitude Estimate?

A Rough Order of Magnitude (ROM) estimate is an estimate given early on, based on the limited available information and high-level concept described in the submitted requirement or user story, the assumptions made on the solution and the risks considered.

The ROM estimate is the least accurate estimate; the PMBOK® Guide Sixth Edition explains *"the differences between [ROM] estimates and actual figures may be as large as 75% more or 25% less."*

The ROM estimate, also referred as Ballpark estimate, is used for long-term portfolio or program planning since the associated requirement or product backlog are typically high-level and not sufficiently described. A ROM estimate is typically useful to create a 1 to 5 years Product Roadmap and communicate to the stakeholders how the product is likely to evolve.

In Scrum, a ROM estimate is best expressed as a T-Shirt Size (XS, S, M, L, etc.).

4.14.2   What is a Preliminary Estimate?

A Preliminary estimate is also an estimate given early in the product or project life, when a high-level logical design is available. The PMBOK® Guide Sixth Edition explains *"the differences between [Preliminary] estimates and actual figures may be as large as 50% more or 15% less."*

Typically, the Preliminary estimate is not used to make a financial commitment but, it assists the customer, the program manager and project manager to better ascertain the required budget to develop the requirement or user story.

In Scrum, a Preliminary estimate can be a T-Shirt Size (XS, S, M, L, etc.) or a Story Point estimate.

4.14.3   What is a Budgetary Estimate?

A Budgetary estimate is a more granular and accurate estimate than the ROM and Preliminary estimates, since the Budgetary estimate may be as large as 25% more or 10% less. It is usually used to allocate funds for a Project or Release, 3 to 6 months ahead of time.

The Budgetary estimate is still a top-down estimate and is often based on past experiences, historical information on project, release costs, initial estimates, and lessons learned. To refine the estimate from Preliminary to Budgetary, the project manager, release manager and product owner collaborate with the solution leads and senior engineers to more granularly define the high-level envisioned solution, which will satisfy the product requirement(s), and review the assumptions and risks considered earlier.

In Scrum, a Budgetary Estimate is given during the Backlog Grooming session, and is typically expressed as a Story Point estimate or in days/hours (when sufficient information is available).

4.14.4 What is a Definitive Estimate?

A Definitive estimate is a bottom-up estimate and is the most accurate estimate the product development team can determine without completing and delivering the product increment. The range of variance between the Definitive estimate and the actual cost is relatively low: 10% more and 5% less.

In Scrum, the Definitive estimate is typically determined during the Sprint Planning and/or Sprint Kick-Off meeting, once the user story or backlog item is decomposed into Tasks (Work Breakdown Structure estimation technique) that can be individually sized. In some cases, the Definitive estimate is ascertained during a special Estimation meeting.

The Definitive estimate is expressed in Level of Effort (hours).

4.14.5 What is a Final Estimate?

A Final estimate is given at the completion or near completion of a Product Increment. It is 100% accurate.

4.15 What does a Typical Day Look like for the Product Owner?

You and I had a long journey exploring and diving into the role and responsibilities of product owner. It's now time to put everything together. Let's go over the typical activities a product owner would perform on a daily, weekly, bi-weekly or regular basis, as illustrated below.

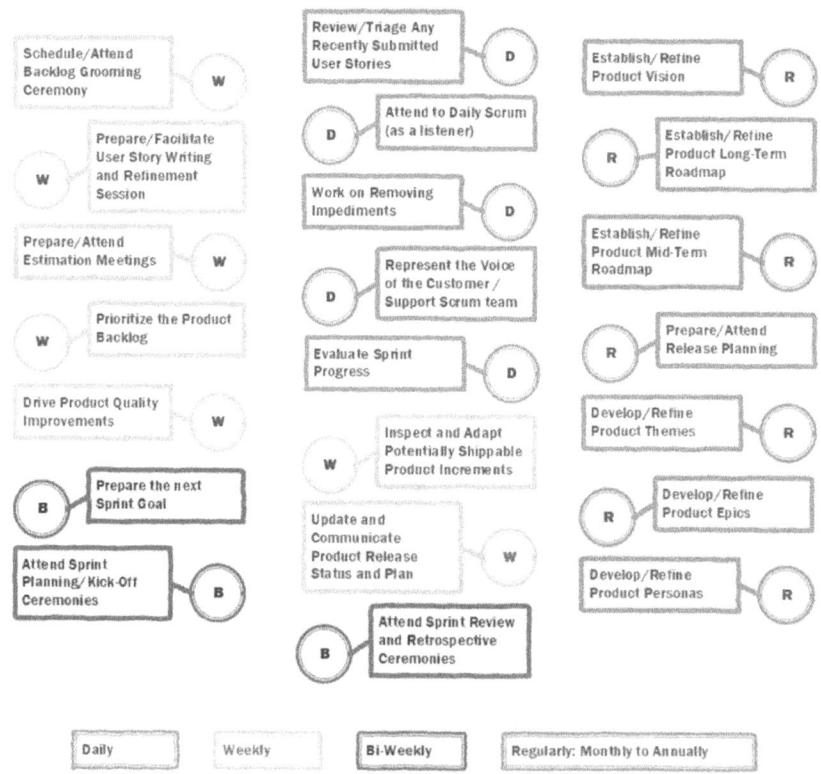

FIGURE 22: ACTIVITIES PERFORMED BY A PRODUCT OWNER

Yes, the product owner will never run out of things to do; and to name only a few of these activities:

- Review and triage any recently submitted user stories
- Schedule and facilitate the Backlog Grooming ceremony
- Prepare, facilitate or support User Story writing and refinement working sessions
- Prepare and attend User Story estimation meetings
- Prioritize the Product Backlog
- Prepare the upcoming sprint goal
- Attend the Sprint Planning and Sprint Kick-off Ceremonies
- Attend the Daily Scrum(s) as a listener
- Support the Scrum team in removing any impediments to progress
- Represent the Voice of Customer, clarifying requirements for the Scrum team
- Evaluate the Sprint progress and work with the team to make any necessary adjustments
- Inspect and adapt the product increments built during the iteration
- Communicate the product release status progress and update the product release plan
- Drive the Product Quality Improvements initiatives
- Attend the Sprint Review and Sprint Retrospective
- Establish and refine the Product Vision and Product Roadmap
- Develop and refine the Product Themes and Epics
- Help developing and refining the Product Personas
- Prepare and attend the Release Planning ceremony

For the product owner, knowing how to manage and prioritize its time is the critical key to success. Some activities must be performed every day, others weekly, while some can be planned and performed on a monthly, quarterly or annual basis.

In his book the 21 Irrefutable Laws of Leadership, John C. Maxwell explained it best: *"Leaders understand that activity is not necessarily accomplishment. To be effective, leaders must order their lives according to these three questions: What is required? What gives the greatest return? And what brings the greatest reward?"*

And because the product owner is a leader too, you must appreciate, embrace and master how to prioritize its own time and activities.

5 Case Study: The Freedom-Crypto Debit Card

Throughout this book, I've leveraged the same case study: a new start-up company wants to build and develop the next generation of debit card: The Freedom-Crypto Debit Card.

This section consolidates the presented examples:

5.1 Business Model Canvas

Key Partners	Key Activities	Value Propositions	Customer Relationships	Customer Segments
Digital Currency Exchange Inc. (DCE) United States Credit Union (USCU)	Acquire, Engage and Retain FCDC members Manage DCE/USCU Transactions	Use digital/crypto currencies to buy what you need. No international exchange rate fee. No hidden fees	Self-Service Online Support User Community	Young Professional Road Warrior Retiree Advertisers
	Key Resources People Cloud Computing Infrastructure		**Channels** Online Social Media	

Cost Structure	Revenue Streams
Fixed: Salary, Product Development, Building lease Variable: DCD/USCU Transactional Fees, Cloud Computing Hosting Solution, Marketing	Fixed: Monthly and Yearly Subscription Fee Variable: Flat Transactional Exchange Fee, Third-Party Advertisement

FIGURE 23: THE FCDC BUSINESS MODEL CANVAS

Reference: Establish the Product Vision, Step 1: Define your Business Model (page 39).

5.2 Problem Statement

[Ideal] Customers should be able to use bitcoins to purchase groceries and shop in Brick and Mortar stores. [Reality] However, only traditional payment instruments, such as cash, check, electronic benefit transfer, debit or credit cards are available to them for making purchases in drugstores and shopping centers. [Issue] Payment through digital cryptocurrencies should be available to customers. [Proposal] The stores' Point-Of-Sale (POS) solutions could be enhanced to integrate cryptocurrency and digital currency exchanges as valid payment instruments.

Reference: Establish the Product Vision, Step 2: Articulate the Problem Statement (page 39).

5.3   Product Vision Statement

"We believe in freedom. Enjoy life with no wall, frontier, and no hidden fee. Buy what you need, when you need it, wherever you live. The Freedom-Crypto Debit Card."

Reference: Establish the Product Vision, Step 3: Ideate Product Vision Statements, and Step 4: Validate your Product Vision (page 41).

5.4   Product Themes

The definition of below product themes comes from the enhanced Telecom Operations Map (eTOM), which is a standard maintained by the TM Forum: https://www.tmforum.org.

The **Customer domain** represents individuals or organizations that obtain products from an enterprise, such as a service provider. It represents of all types of contact with the customer, the management of the relationship, and the administration of customer data. Customer also includes customer bills for products, collection of payment, overdue accounts, and the billing inquiries and adjustments made as a result of inquiries.

The **Engaged Party domain** encompasses planning of strategies for Engaged Parties, handling of all types of contact with Engaged Parties, the management of the relationship, and the administration of Engaged Parties data. It also supports a variety of interactions such as requests, bills, disputes and inquiries associated with an Engaged Party. While Engaged Parties are third parties assisting with meeting an Enterprise's *customer needs, they represent a myriad of potential roles in the value fabric. Engaged parties play a key role in an end customer transaction.*

Reference: Determine the Product Themes (page 43)

5.5   Product Epics

We limited our discussions on how people can use a `Freedom-Crypto Debit Card (FCDC)`, and came-up with a few stories:

(1) As a `FCDC holder,` I want to `withdraw cash from an ATM (selling available bitcoins)` so that `I can purchase items at any stores.`

(2) As a `FCDC holder,` I want to `deposit cash into my account at any ATM` so that `I can purchase additional bitcoins.`

(3) As a `FCDC holder,` I want to `use my debit card at any stores` so that `I can purchase grocery or other items.`

(4) As a `FCDC holder,` I want to `make online purchases using my debit card` so that `I can benefit from online product offerings and special deals.`

(5) As a `FCDC holder,` I want to `make online deposits into my account` so that `I can purchase additional bitcoins.`

Let's not forget that an epic should also have clear acceptance criteria. For example, let's use the epic (1). The acceptance criteria can be as follows:

1. `The FCDC holder has a cryptocurrency or digital exchange account.`

2. `The total value available in the digital exchange account is greater than the amount to be withdrawn.`

3. `The FCDC holder has swiped and entered a valid PIN.`

4. `The requested amount and withdrawal fees were debited from the account.`

5. `The ATM has dispensed the requested cash amount to the FCDC holder.`

6. The FCDC holder has received an email with the detailed transactions.

Reference: Determine the Product Epics (page 46).

5.6 Product Personas

We can easily craft three different personas who would be interested in owning and using the infamous FCDC!

- **The retired couple:** Patrick and Lenah have been married for 30 years. Patrick is retired and Lenah will soon be. They invested in cryptocurrency several years ago. They decided to acquire a Freedom-Crypto Debit Card to limit their future 401k annual distribution, thus minimizing federal and state taxes, while maintaining their current lifestyle.

- **The young professional:** Yin has recently purchased a few bitcoins but has rapidly change his mind due to the market high volatility. He got a Freedom-Crypto Debit Card to slowly get rid of his digital assets while still hoping for the market to settle down and become bullish again.

- **The road warrior:** Malika has been day-trading and investing in digital currencies for several years. She loves traveling and exploring new countries. But she also wants to minimize the steep banking and currency exchanges fees that typically rhyme with traveling abroad. She obtained a Freedom-Crypto Debit Card specifically to make purchases during her travels and stop worrying about any hidden fees.

	Persona's Details	Persona's Goals
The Retired Couple Patrick and Lenah	• Patrick is 64 years old, Lenah 62. • They've been married for 30 years and have 2 children and 1 grand-daughter. • Patrick worked for 26 years for the same company and retired 2 years ago. • Lenah is currently employed but plans on retiring in 2 months. • They invested in cryptocurrency 5 years ago to diversify their portfolio.	• They want to use their cryptocurrency assets to make daily purchases and minimize their 401k annual distribution.
The Young Professional Yin	• Yin is 27 years old. • He graduated 3 years ago with a BA in Business Administration Management. • He works for a leading consulting firm. • He actively follows the financial news and decided to purchase five bitcoins.	• Yin no longer believes in bitcoins because of today's market volatility. He wants to slowly liquidate his assets while still hoping the market improves.
The Road Warrior Malika	• Malika is 41 years old. • She works part-time as a Pharmacist. • She's been day-trading and investing in digital currencies for 10 years. • She frequently travels internationally to explore different scenery, culture, and cuisine.	• Malika wants to avoid currency exchange and banking fees while traveling.

FIGURE 24: THE FCDC PRODUCT PERSONAS

Reference: Develop the Product Personas (page 49).

5.7   User Story Mapping

Customer Domain				
As a FCDC holder, I want to withdraw cash from an ATM (selling available bitcoins) so that I can purchase items at any stores.	As a FCDC holder, I want to deposit cash into my account at any ATM so that I purchase additional bitcoins.	As a FCDC holder, I want to use my debit card at any stores so that I can purchase grocery or other items.	As a FCDC holder, I want to make online purchases using my debit card so that I can benefit from online product offering and special deals.	As a FCDC holder, I want to deposit online payments into my account so that I purchase additional bitcoins.

Minimum Viable Product

As a FCDC holder, I want to access USA Credit Unit ATMs to withdraw cash from my available digital currency account(s).

Future Product Increments

As a FCDC holder, I want to access any ATMs to withdraw cash from my available digital currency account(s).

As a FCDC holder, I want to access USA Credit Unit ATMs to purchase additional digital currencies from cash.

As a FCDC holder, I want to access any ATMs to purchase additional digital currencies from cash.

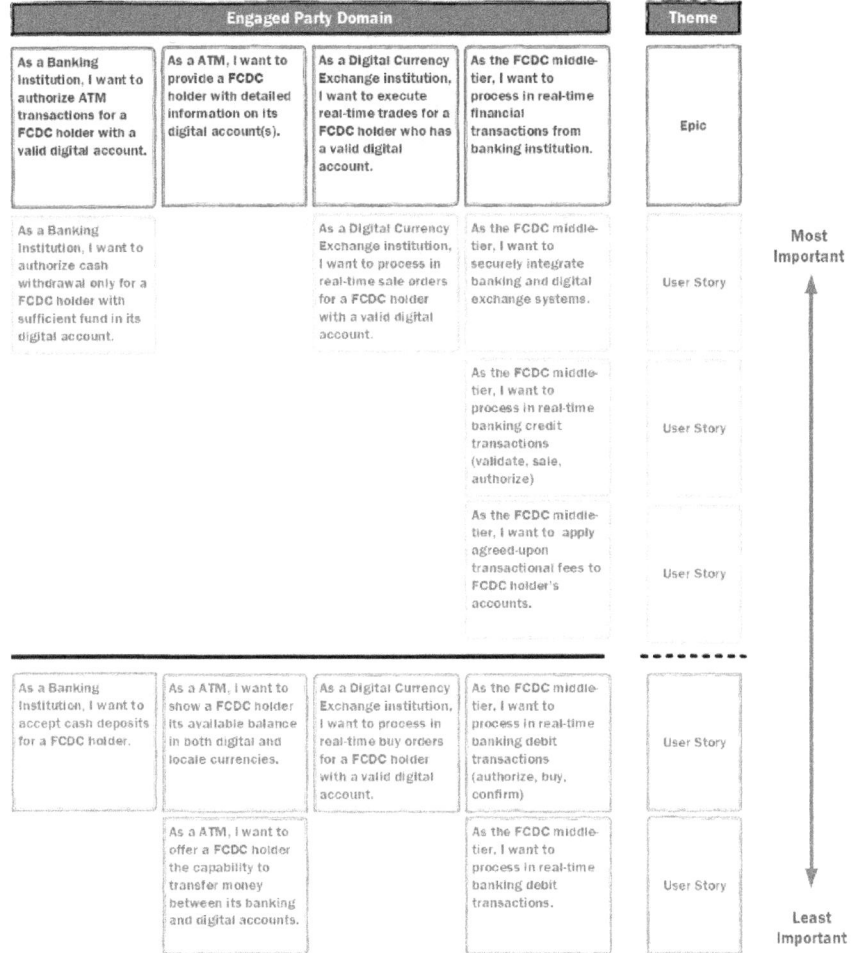

FIGURE 25: THE FCDC USER-STORY MAP

Reference: Plan the Next Product Release (using User Story Mapping) (page 62).

5.8 Product Release (using User-Story Mapping)

	Sprint M1	Sprint M2	Sprint M3
Freedom-Crypto Debit Card (FCDC) Product Development Scrum Team	As FCDC, I want to securely integrate banking and digital exchange systems.	As FCDC, I want to map a FC debit card with an DCE account	As FCDC, I want to submit to USCU a cash deposit request to a valid USCA account
	As FCDC, I want to enable secured submission of trade orders to DCE	As FCDC, I want to submit to DCE a sale orders for a valid DCE account	As FCDC, I want to validate a sale order to DCE and cash deposit from DCE to FCDC account
	As FCDC, I want to enable secured submission of banking instructions to USCU	As FCDC, I want to map a FC debit card with an USCU bank account	
Digital Currency Exchange Inc. (DCE) Product Development Scrum Team	As DCE, I want to enable secured reception of trade orders from FCDC	As DCE, I want to process in real-time sale orders for a FCDC holder with a valid digital account.	As DCE, I want to validate a sale order from FCDC and cash transfer to FCDC account
USA Credit Unit (USCU) Product Development Scrum Team	As DCE, I want to enable secured reception of banking instructions from FCDC		As USCA, I want to accept from FCDC a cash deposit in a valid USCA account

Sprint M4	Sprint M5	Sprint M6
As FCDC, I want to process in real-time banking credit transactions (validate, sale, authorize)	As the FCDC middle-tier, I want to apply agreed-upon transactional fees to FCDC holder's accounts.	As a FCDC holder, I want to access USA Credit Unit ATMs to withdraw cash from my available digital currency account(s).
	As FCDC, I want to validate end-to-end transaction from DCE sale order to cash deposit to USCU account	
	As DCE, I want to assist in end-to-end validation from FCDC	
As USCA, I want to authorize cash withdrawal for a FCDC holder with sufficient fund in its digital account.	As USCA, I want to assist in end-to-end validation from FCDC	

Freedom-Crypto Debit Card (FCDC) Product Development Scrum Team

Digital Currency Exchange Inc. (DCE) Product Development Scrum Team

USA Credit Unit (USCU) Product Development Scrum Team

FIGURE 26: THE FCDC RELEASE 0 USER STORY MAP BOARD

Reference: Plan the Next Product Release (using User Story Mapping): Develop the Release Plan (page 67).

5.9 Product Roadmap (using User-Story Mapping)

	H1Y1
	Release 1

Customer Domain

As a FCDC holder, I want to withdraw cash from an ATM (selling available bitcoins) so that I can purchase items at any stores.

As a FCDC holder, I want to access USA Credit Unit ATMs to withdraw cash from my available digital currency account(s).

As a FCDC holder, I want to deposit cash into my account at any ATM so that I purchase additional bitcoins.

Engaged Party Domain

As a Banking Institution, I want to authorize ATM transactions for a FCDC holder with a valid digital account.

As a Banking Institution, I want to authorize cash withdrawal only for a FCDC holder with sufficient fund in its digital account.

As a ATM, I want to provide a FCDC holder with detailed information on its digital account(s).

As a Digital Currency Exchange institution, I want to execute real-time trades for a FCDC holder who has a valid digital account.

As a Digital Currency Exchange institution, I want to process in real-time sale orders for a FCDC holder with a valid digital account.

As the FCDC middle-tier, I want to process in real-time financial transactions from banking institution.

As the FCDC middle-tier, I want to securely integrate banking and digital exchange systems.

As the FCDC middle-tier, I want to process in real-time banking credit transactions (validate, sale, authorize).

As the FCDC middle-tier, I want to apply agreed-upon transactional fees to FCDC holder's accounts.

	Q3H1	Q4H1	Y2
	Release 2	**Release 3**	**Release N**

	Q3H1 – Release 2	Q4H1 – Release 3	Y2 – Release N
Customer Domain	As a FCDC holder, I want to withdraw cash from an ATM (selling available bitcoins) so that I can purchase items at any stores.		As a FCDC holder, I want to access any ATMs to withdraw cash from my available digital currency account(s).
	As a FCDC holder, I want to deposit cash into my account at any ATM so that I purchase additional bitcoins.	As a FCDC holder, I want to access USA Credit Unit ATMs to purchase additional digital currencies from cash.	As a FCDC holder, I want to access any ATMs to purchase additional digital currencies from cash.
Engaged Party Domain	As a Banking Institution, I want to authorize ATM transactions for a FCDC holder with a valid digital account.	As a Banking Institution, I want to accept cash deposits for a FCDC holder.	
	As a ATM, I want to provide a FCDC holder with detailed information on its digital account(s).	As a ATM, I want to show a FCDC holder its available balance in both digital and locale currencies.	As a ATM, I want to offer a FCDC holder the capability to transfer money between its banking and digital accounts.
	As a Digital Currency Exchange institution, I want to execute real-time trades for a FCDC holder who has a valid digital account.	As a Digital Currency Exchange institution, I want to process in real-time buy orders for a FCDC holder with a valid digital account.	
	As the FCDC middle-tier, I want to process in real-time financial transactions from banking institution.	As the FCDC middle-tier, I want to process in real-time banking debit transactions (authorize, buy, confirm)	

FIGURE 27: THE FCDC PRODUCT ROADMAP USING USER-STORY MAPPING

Reference: Assist in Establishing the Product Roadmap (page 70).

5.10 Product Roadmap (using Scenario Planning)

Step 1: Conduct an Academic Research

- Policies and Regulations:
  - Privacy over customer personal sensitive information
  - Privacy around customer financial transactions
  - Protection of biometric digital identities
  - Regulation of traditional banking institutions
  - International Regulation around cryptocurrency and digital currency exchanges
  - Country-specific bans on cryptocurrency exchanges
- Industry:
  - Rise or decline of cryptocurrencies
  - Adoption level of cryptocurrencies by traditional banking institutions
  - New entrants in payment processing and solutions
  - Rise or decline of peer-to-peer payments
  - Merger and Acquisition in the Banking and Tech industries
- Technology:
  - Adoption level of online and mobile banking services
  - Technology innovation supporting banking activities
  - Agreement on a Common Information and Data Exchange Model for the banking industry
  - Evolution and adoption of blockchain technology
  - Cybersecurity threat and attack on digital currency exchanges

Let's now go over what we do know and do not know about the driving forces that could affect tomorrow:

- Policies and Regulations:
  - Would new or revised policies attract or prevent new entrants?
  - Would regulations and policies be centrally enforced?

- o Would new or revised regulations reduce the number of cryptocurrency and digital currency holders?
- **Industry:**
  - o How many people will be using cryptocurrencies?
  - o How many traditional banks will adopt digital currencies?
  - o How many digital currencies will be created?
  - o How many digital currency exchanges will be developed and participate?
  - o Would new payment or retail use cases surface?
- **Technology:**
  - o Would multiple common information models (CIM) be defined?
  - o Would the different data exchange standards be interoperable?
  - o How would cybersecurity requirements further impact banking and digital currency exchange systems?
  - o Who would hold the digital wallets enabling electronic transactions?
  - o How would cloud-computing systems and storage solutions accelerate deployment of a product?
  - o Which technology stack will lower the overall solution cost of ownership?
  - o How fast would ATM and POS be able to integrate cryptocurrencies?
  - o Would all digital currency exchanges support real-time transactions?

Let's consider the dynamics influencing both trends and uncertainties:

- **Policies and Regulations:**
  - o Elect an influencer in the company board of directors
  - o Participate in public panels and legislative discussions
  - o Contribute to the digital currency standards
  - o Include regulators in key business decisions
- **Industry:**
  - o Collaborate with traditional banks and credit units

- o Help banking and financial institutions to develop business cases so that they can integrate digital currencies in their product portfolio
- o Be acquired by a financial institution
- o Merge with a digital currency exchange
- Technology:
  - o Acquire a start-up in payments processing
  - o Understand cybersecurity technologies
  - o Ramp-up on common information model and data exchange standards
  - o Train on cloud-computing systems

Step 2: Inject some Practicality into your Assumptions

Draw on a whiteboard a matrix with two axes: the vertical axis measures the impact on the product, and the horizontal axis measures the predictability and uncertainty.

Stricter regulations are put in place around cryptocurrencies exchanges and payment instruments

Some banks and financial institutions adopt digital currencies

Use of cryptocurrencies is limited online retail and peer-to-peer payments.

Cyber-Security and Cloud-Computing systems begin adopting blockchain technologies

Limited number of new entrants in cryptocurrency payment instruments

Regulations support cryptocurrencies exchanges and payment instruments

Banks and financial institutions adopt digital currencies

Cryptocurrencies cross the chasm and become a new standard for retail and peer-to-peer payments.

Cyber-Security and Cloud-Computing systems fully embrace blockchain technologies

Limited number of new entrants in cryptocurrency payment instruments

Stricter regulations are put in place around cryptocurrencies exchanges and payment instruments

Limited number of banks and financial institutions adopt digital currencies

Use of cryptocurrencies is limited to peer-to-peer payments.

Cyber-Security and Cloud Computing systems adopt some blockchain technologies

Large number of new entrants in cryptocurrency payment instruments

Regulations make cryptocurrencies exchanges illegal

Use of cryptocurrencies is marginalized

Cyber-Security and Cloud-Computing systems don't embrace blockchain technologies

Predictable

Uncertain

Negative/Low Impacts

FIGURE 28: THE FCDC SCENARIO PLANNING MATRIX

Step 3: Develop the Scenario Narratives

Step 4: Determine the Product Directions

Reference: Assist in Establishing the Product Roadmap, Establish the Long-term Product Roadmap (page 74)

5.11 Sprint Goal

Sprint M1 is about enabling the financial transactions between Freedom-Crypto Debit Card (FCDC), Digital Currency Exchange Inc. (DCE) and ATMs operated by USA Credit Unit (USCU).

Sprint M2 is to submit a Sale Order to DCE so that a FCDC customer can withdraw cash at an ATM operated by USCU.

Reference: Manage the Sprint: Define the Sprint Goal (page 81)

5.12 Sprint Backlog

ID	Description	Priority	Story Points
FCDC01	As FCDC, I want to securely integrate banking and digital exchange systems.	1. Must	7
FCDC01.T1	Define and Obtain agreement on the API contract between FCDC, DCE and USCU	1. Must	9
FCDC01.T2	Implement API contract to DCE and USCU	1. Must	21
FCDC02	As FCDC, I want to enable secured submission of trade orders to DCE	1. Must	5
FCDC02.T1	Define and Obtain agreement with DCE on payload and encryption methodology	1. Must	9
FCDC02.T2	Implement payload and encryption to DCE for trade orders	2. Should	13
FCDC03	As FCDC, I want to enable secured submission of banking instructions to USCU	1. Must	5
FCDC03.T1	Implement payload and encryption to USCU for banking instructions	2. Should	9
FCDC04	As DCE, I want to enable secured reception of trade orders from FCDC	1. Must	5
FCDC04.T1	Handle trader order requests from FCDC	2. Should	5

TABLE 6: THE **FCDC** SPRINT BACKLOG

Reference: Manage the Sprint: Review the Sprint Backlog (page 83)

This page is intentionally left blank.

And, Coming Soon....

Photo Credits

Cover photo by Ty'Onah Gallman, licensed under the Creative Commons Attribution 2.0 Generic license.

URL: https://www.flickr.com/photos/110159196@N05/

License: https://creativecommons.org/licenses/by/2.0/

Photo	Credits and URL
	Credit: Icon made by Freepik from www.flaticon.com License: https://file000.flaticon.com/downloads/license/license.pdf Link: https://www.flaticon.com/free-icon/couple_437519
	Credit: Icon made by Freepik from www.flaticon.com License: https://file000.flaticon.com/downloads/license/license.pdf URL: https://www.flaticon.com/free-icon/man_417777
	Credit: Icon made by Vectors Market from www.flaticon.com License: https://file000.flaticon.com/downloads/license/license.pdf URL: https://www.flaticon.com/free-icon/clerk_607406
	Credit: Icon made by Eucalyp from www.flaticon.com License: https://file000.flaticon.com/downloads/license/license.pdf URL: https://www.flaticon.com/free-icon/graphic-design_181378
	Credit: Icon made by Becris from www.flaticon.com License: https://file000.flaticon.com/downloads/license/license.pdf URL: https://www.flaticon.com/free-icon/empathy_860387

Photo	Credits and URL
	Credit: Icon made by Skyclick from www.flaticon.com License: https://file000.flaticon.com/downloads/license/license.pdf URL: https://www.flaticon.com/free-icon/creative-idea_902744
	Credit: Icon made by Smartline from www.flaticon.com License: https://file000.flaticon.com/downloads/license/license.pdf URL: https://www.flaticon.com/free-icon/prototype_155361
	Credit: Icon made by Eucalyp from www.flaticon.com License: https://file000.flaticon.com/downloads/license/license.pdf URL: https://www.flaticon.com/free-icon/pros-and-cons_181379
	Credit: Icon made by geotatah from www.flaticon.com License: https://file000.flaticon.com/downloads/license/license.pdf URL: https://www.flaticon.com/free-icon/customers_994712
	Credit: Icon made by Becris from www.flaticon.com License: https://file000.flaticon.com/downloads/license/license.pdf URL: https://www.flaticon.com/free-icon/leadership_860380
	Credit: Icon made by prettycons from www.flaticon.com License: https://file000.flaticon.com/downloads/license/license.pdf URL: https://www.flaticon.com/free-icon/network_978012
	Credit: Icon made by Pause08 from www.flaticon.com License: https://file000.flaticon.com/downloads/license/license.pdf URL: https://www.flaticon.com/free-icon/flow-chart_858164
	Credit: Icon made by Freepik from www.flaticon.com License: https://file000.flaticon.com/downloads/license/license.pdf URL: https://www.flaticon.com/free-icon/business-statistics-sketch_59767
	Credit: Icon made by Pixel perfect from www.flaticon.com License: https://file000.flaticon.com/downloads/license/license.pdf URL: https://www.flaticon.com/free-icon/fingerprint_273989
	Credit: Icon made by Freepik from www.flaticon.com License: https://file000.flaticon.com/downloads/license/license.pdf URL: https://www.flaticon.com/free-icon/relationship_1005613

This page is intentionally left blank.

www.ingramcontent.com/pod-product-compliance
Lightning Source LLC
Chambersburg PA
CBHW071301220526
45468CB00001B/225